THE SHADOW IN THE HOROSCOPE

Five Essays on
Jung's Concept of The Shadow

THE SHADOW IN THE HOROSCOPE

Five Essays on
Jung's Concept of The Shadow

GLENN PERRY

AAP Press

East Hampton, CT • www.aaperry.com

ISBN 10: 0615634176

ISBN-13: 978-0615634173

To Ruth

CONTENTS

TABLE OF FIGURES

ACKNOWLEDGMENTS

I would like to express my gratitude to Twink McKenney for her visionary skills in helping design the cover of *The Shadow in the Horoscope*. Also, I have been fortunate to have Gina Bostian's expertise in formatting the book and for her support and encouragement along the way. Thanks are also due to the entire Design Team at Createspace for their earnest determination in getting the book to press expeditiously. Finally, I want to thank my many friends and colleagues in the astrological community for their encouragement in bringing this manuscript to print.

INTRODUCTION

In Prague on August 16th, 2006, the planet Pluto was demoted by the International Astronomical Union to the rather ignominious status of 'dwarf planet'. This was due to the fact that Pluto allegedly had not cleared the region of space around its orbit of large objects, as had the other eight planetary bodies of our solar system. While this charge was hotly disputed at the Prague conference, Caltech researcher Mike Brown eagerly pronounced to reporters via teleconference that "Pluto is dead."

Had astrologers been at the conference they might have informed Brown that you cannot kill death, which is what Pluto has traditionally signified within the field of astrology since its discovery in 1930. Although controversy continues to rage over Pluto's demotion, and many astronomers are petitioning to have the decision overturned, it is perhaps fitting that Pluto should be demoted and relegated to inferior status in the pantheon of gods. Astrologically, Pluto is analogous to Lucifer, who was cast out of heaven. Pluto is lord of the underworld, of Hades, and thus of the frightening, reprehensible parts of the psyche that figuratively speaking have been cast into our personal hells. Pluto has other meanings, too, such as healing and transformation, but these can only be understood in the context of its association with things dark, shadowy, and wounded.

When Pluto is bound up with other planets in the chart, especially by what astrologers call "hard aspects" (angles of 90, 150, or 180 degrees), the psychological functions these planets represent are often abducted into the underworld and cast into shadow. They are devalued, "demoted" as it were, and regarded as dangerous, potentially painful, and thus feared. In effect, they become ostracized. Psychologically, we call this repression, but it amounts to the same thing.

Archetypally, Pluto is depicted as the dark stranger, the mysterious outsider who doesn't belong, like Clint Eastwood – "the man with no name" – drifting into town from the high plains. In these early Eastwood films, he inevitably transforms the town by killing all the bad guys. Pluto not only wounds, it also cleanses, purges, and heals. How odd that Pluto was actually demoted for *not* purging its neighborhood of other bodies. One suspects the astronomers have made a mistake.

The dark lord is strange and often scary precisely because it doesn't belong. It resides at the outer perimeter of the solar system, the border of the unknown, and is the only planet that penetrates the boundary of another planet – Neptune – by occasionally moving inside its orbit. That's what Pluto does: *penetrate*. Pluto' orbital characteristics are substantially different from the other planets, all of which follow nearly circular orbits around the Sun on the ecliptic. In contrast, Pluto's orbit is highly inclined relative to the ecliptic, which means that Pluto dives deeply down into the area substantially *below* the ecliptic where it remains for nearly half its 248 year orbit. That's a long time in the underworld, even for Pluto.

Metaphorically speaking, all of this is consistent with Pluto's demotion to inferior status as a dwarf planet. Again, this is what we do to those "plutonized" parts of the psyche that we cannot accept, which are often associated with trauma, wounding, and shame. When projected, Pluto appears as "the enemy" — people who are dehumanized precisely because they are perceived as threatening. Clearly, Pluto's demotion by astronomers to the status of a dwarf planet has absolutely no impact on its astrological usage or significance. If anything, the demotion of Pluto merely reinforces its archetypal status as lord of the underworld.

This book is about Jung's concept of the shadow and its close association with Pluto. As mentioned, Pluto is naturally associated with things dark and shadowy. It also symbolizes the wounded-healer archetype, which necessarily has two poles: wounded and healer. When Pluto forms a hard aspect to another planet, that planet's functions tend to be split into opposite halves and mixed with the wounded-healer archetype. The dark, projected side appears to be wounded, while the light, inflated side feels imbued with healing potential. Because a split archetype tries persistently to restore its original integrity, the individual becomes obsessed with transforming or destroying whatever has been projected. Yet, if wholeness is to be restored, such planets require healing from the inside. In so doing, extremism is mitigated and buried potentials recovered.

In this book, five different manifestations of the shadow are explored. Chapter 1 examines the astrologer's shadow, which is associated with delusions of omniscience—a vulnerability to which astrologers are especially susceptible. Chapter 2 provides an astrological case history of Dr. Laura Schlessinger, the infamous talk show shrink who may embody the dark side of the helping professions. In myth and cinema, perhaps there is no better example of the shadow than Darth Vader, whose fall and ultimate redemption is dramatically illustrated in the chart of George Lucas, our subject of Chapter 3. Chapter 4 explores another shadowy figure of cinematic magic, King Kong, a uniquely 20th century version of the Pluto and Persephone myth. Finally, we explore the Saturn-Pluto opposition of 2001-2002, which strikingly illustrates the collective dimension of the shadow as manifest in the war on terrorism that reached a crescendo during this period.

So, turn out the lights, curl up on your couch with some popcorn and a dimly lit candle, and read about these strange denizens of our astrological underworld—shadowy astrologers, wounded healers, dark fathers, erotic monsters, and mad dog terrorists.

~**Glenn Perry**
Haddam Neck, CT
April 10, 2012

Chapter One

The Astrologer's Shadow

THE ALL-KNOWING, SUPREMELY WISE CONSULTANT

Why did I decide to become an astrologer? I've reflected on that fateful decision many times. On the surface, it does not seem a wise choice. Astrology is discredited in our culture and astrologers are largely regarded as fools or frauds. Only a few make a decent living at it, and even then must be willing to suffer the ignominy of succeeding in a profession that is regularly attacked by leaders in the scientific and academic community.*

In the remainder of this chapter, I'd like to explore my motivations for choosing astrology as a career. In so doing, I hope to shed light on a problem that I suspect is endemic within our profession. Choice of a career in astrology may actually be symptomatic of certain psychological issues and wounds. At the

---

* In 2001, Kepler College of Astrological Arts and Sciences was attacked in several newspaper articles. "By granting Kepler College formal accreditation," wrote John Silber, chancellor of Boston University, "the Higher Education Board of the state of Washington stands exposed as ignorant, foolish and contemptuous of the public interest." Likewise, Alvin Kwiram, University of Washington Vice Provost for Research, equated Kepler with "a college of quack medicine." Silber's article appeared May 16, 2001 in the *Boston Herald*. Kwiram was quoted in the Seattle Post-Intelligencer on July 23, 2001 in an article titled, "Astrology school sets off controversy."

same time, these issues may be reflected in the astrological chart. If this is true, then our charts can point us in the direction of healing the very wounds that impede our success as astrologers.

SHADOW ISSUES

My own experience in psychotherapy has taught me that everything we do is psychologically motivated. A particularly important factor in motivation is what Jung called the *shadow*. Whatever one feels intensely negative toward is usually bound up with shadow issues. For example, if one cannot tolerate aggressiveness, then aggression (Mars) may be part of one's shadow.

The shadow has both a collective and a personal dimension. On a collective level, it can be embodied in anything that the larger community regards as reprehensible, primitive, or inferior. This can be certain kind of actions, such as drug dealing, various out groups, like gays or minorities, and specific belief systems, like astrology. Because astrology is a throwback to earlier, pre-scientific cultures, it represents an archaic ideology that was banished from university curriculums by the end of the 17th century. As such, it signifies a shadow doctrine whose continued existence is threatening to proponents of the scientific world-view. Needless to say, astrology is *persona non grata* in our schools and universities.

The personal dimension of the shadow has to do with psychic potentialities of which the individual is unaware. These include inferior characteristics that the ego renounces, e.g., greed, laziness, or lust. Such qualities are relegated to the unconscious and cast into darkness. Jung's metaphor of "shadow" is apt, for when we identify exclusively with the light side of our natures, i.e. our ideal self, traits, or accomplishments, we are identifying only with what we *want* to be. This of necessity constellates a shadow at the opposite pole: what we *don't want to be.* By rigidly focusing upon the good, we ignore or repudiate certain negative potentialities. Success coaches have a common refrain: *focus on the positive.* Yet, this can be a dangerous half-truth that creates serious problems whenever the shadow erupts. Self-sabotage, hatred of others, and malevolent intentions are just a few of the problems that derive from an unconscious shadow.

Jung regarded the shadow as first and foremost a *moral* problem. Unless one has the courage to face one's shadow it will invariably be projected. In so doing, we demonize in others what we cannot face in ourselves. First there is a tendency to selectively attend to manifestations of one's shadow as it appears on the outside. If we abhor weakness in ourselves, we will be preoccupied with it in our companions. As Jung put it, "Projections change the world into the replica of one's unknown face".[1]

Second, there will be an impulse to attack, derogate, or reform people that carry our shadow. Our criticism may masquerade as righteous indignation, but underneath it is more akin to hatred. It is exceedingly difficult to have empathy for qualities that one has rejected in oneself. Whenever we are possessed by strong negative emotion (anger, revulsion, or vengeance), very likely we are in the grip of our shadow. Lack of compassion is almost always symptomatic of a shadow problem. In fact, projection of the shadow underlies most of what we call *evil*.

Related to evil is the impulse to seek power *over* the thing that one fears. Abuse of power operates on a continuum, from the more benign forms of manipulation and coercion to the more destructive variants of oppression, tyranny, and murder. "Where love rules," said Jung, "there is no will to power; and where power predominates, there love is lacking. The one is the shadow of the other."[2]

Human beings have an innate tendency to condemn on the outside qualities they repudiate on the inside. For example, if a preacher is sexually repressed, he rails against "sinners" that are unable to control their lust. He condemns others at his own peril, however, for he has set the stage for becoming the thing that he most abhors. This is a theme in countless stories. The more one struggles against evil by striving to be *good*, the more one becomes vulnerable to possession by the dark side. Jung referred to this as *enantiodromia*—the tendency for things to revert to their opposite. He observed that if one side of a pair of opposites becomes excessively predominant in the personality, it is likely to turn into its contrary. This is because the psyche has an innate tropism toward balance, or wholeness. Robert Lewis Stevenson's immortal tale, *Dr. Jeckyl and Mr. Hyde,* is a prime example. In seeking to serve humanity as the pure and noble physician, Dr. Jeckyl constellated a powerful shadow that sporadically seized control of his personality, turning him into the corrupt, ignoble Mr. Hyde.

The shadow is especially powerful during situations of crisis. If someone is under extreme stress or suffers a major disappointment, the shadow steps in with little resistance from a weakened ego. Qualities that we *thought* we had overcome suddenly rear their ugly head. A recovering alcoholic goes on a binge. A fundamentalist Christian collapses into promiscuity. Such "slips" remind us that the negative elements of one's character are never eliminated entirely. They simply withdraw into unconsciousness and reside in a latent state, like a virus waiting for the immune system to be sufficiently weakened so that they can wreak havoc once more.

Shadow work requires turning away from the light side and looking backwards into the silhouette cast by one's ideal self.* Only then can we see and remember what we are trying to leave behind. Often these are traits that we have struggled to eliminate from

---

* Connie Sweig and Jeremiah Abrams coined the term shadow-work in their book *Meeting The Shadow.* It refers to the continuing effort to develop a creative relationship with the shadow.

our natures—avarice, arrogance, cruelty, dogmatism, selfishness, dependency, or other such negative qualities. Their memory haunts us, however, for they represent an atavistic tendency that we have pledged ourselves to overcome. Facing and integrating our dark side can reduce the intensity of such issues, though we may never eradicate them completely. True goodness does not simply abolish badness; it *forgives* it, first in oneself and then in others. "One does not become enlightened by imagining figures of light," says Jung, "but by making the darkness conscious."[3]

It bears repeating that everyone has a shadow. The more one denies it, the blacker and denser it becomes. Rejection of the shadow tends to flatten the personality into a two-dimensional façade—a "cardboard angel" in the words of Sheldon Kopp. Loss of depth, passion, and erotic intensity is symptomatic of shadow repression.

Conversely, acceptance of the dark side gives the personality a full-bodied, three-dimensional quality. One becomes more authentic, sexually appealing, and capable of spontaneity, humor, strong emotion, and deep insights. To the extent that one integrates the shadow, there is also less fear of its external manifestations. And in the absence of fear, one gains power—not power *over* others, but power that comes from personal integrity. "Shadow work," says Abrams "leads to a practice I refer to as the pursuit of the unhypocritical life, which some might call living with integrity."[4] Integrity connotes a willingness to suffer or die for the deepest truth of one's being. Conversely, neurotic fear implies the opposite: cowardice and self-betrayal.

FINDING THE SHADOW IN THE CHART

In astrology, there is no single factor that signifies the shadow, but a good place to start is by examining Pluto's sign, house, and aspects.* As the planet that symbolizes death and rebirth, Pluto necessarily deals with processes of transformation. By integrating whatever resides in one's personal underworld, the individual must be willing to die, not literally, but figuratively. Such processes are associated with self-renewal and healing. Everything we've been saying about the shadow—its association with fear and loathing, repression of disowned parts, projection, demonization of others, subjugation of the enemy, power trips and power struggles, possession, disempowerment, and loss of personal integrity—all derive from a failure to integrate Pluto. In effect, an unintegrated Pluto is synonymous with the shadow.

Like the shadow, Pluto never exists in a pure state, for it is always associated with *something*. If Pluto forms a hard aspect to the Moon, it tends to abduct lunar functions into the underworld. Pluto casts a shadow over *whatever* it touches. Here lays our wound, but also our capacity to heal. As Liz Greene put it, "The shadow is both the awful thing that needs redemption, and the suffering redeemer who can provide it."[5]

Prior to transformation, psychic wounds are projected. Once projected, they are responded to with either fearful avoidance or hostile confrontation; it is a "flight or fight" response. Pluto's all-or-nothing intensity is due to its association with pain and death. Because the stakes are high, we take it to the limit. This process is motivated by (1) a chronic fear that we are not going to get something we need, (2) a perception that the need is critical, and (3) a conviction that any attempt to satisfy the need endangers our safety. In a word, Pluto equates to *crisis*.

---

* One might also look at planets in the 8th house, planets in Scorpio, and planets that form a closing quincunx. An aspect derives its meaning from the nature of the sign to which it corresponds. As the 8th sign of the zodiac, Scorpio is 150 degrees from a closing of a 360-degree cycle. The closing quincunx is a Scorpio angle in that it constitutes the last 150 degrees in the synodic cycle between two planets. Planets in closing quincunx are having a Scorpio dialogue; they tend to experience each other as mutually wounding, painful, and difficult to integrate. In effect, they are shadows for one another.

When situations are critical, there is a tendency to go to extremes, which by definition means the outermost point at one end of a continuum. Extreme behavior is immoderate; it extends far beyond the norm. Either of the two things situated at opposite ends of a range constitutes *the extreme,* e.g., the extremes of boiling and freezing. In mathematics, it's the maximum or minimum of a function. When we talk about extremes, then, we are implicitly talking about polarities. To appreciate this, consider that every archetype contains a natural polarity. For example, every warrior (Mars) battles a foe, every lover (Venus) loves a beloved, every savior (Neptune) saves a victim, and every performer (Sun) entertains an audience.* These are archetypal *roles* or characters. If one pole is constellated in the outside world, the opposite pole is constellated internally.

Archetypes also constitute *psychological* polarities, e.g., bliss and grief (Neptune), security and insecurity (Venus), or acceptance and rejection (Moon). Under normal circumstances, both poles are contained within the same individual. If a person is in balance, s/he can empathize with either side of the archetype. One can identify with warrior *and* foe (Mars), intimacy *and* distance (Venus), bliss *and* tragedy (Neptune), and so on.

It is not easy for the human psyche to bear the tension of polarities. The ego loves clarity, "I am this, but not *that.*" It tries to eradicate the inner ambivalence. This tendency toward the nonequivocal is exacerbated when Pluto aspects a planet by hard angle (0°, 90°, 150°, 180°). That planet becomes associated with pain and fear such that *any* expression of the archetype feels

---

* While every planet contains a natural polarity, these are not reducible to only two roles. Rather, there are a variety of ways in which a single archetype can be split into opposite halves. The Sun, for example, is not only performer-audience, but also hero-beneficiary, romancer-romanced, and king-subject. Each of these opposing roles are Leonian, but one tends to be more active—performer, hero, romancer, king—while the other tends to be more passive—audience (fan, admirer), beneficiary, romanced, and subject.

dangerous. Once fear infects the planet, the archetype is split and the individual can only identify with one side of a natural polarity. Pathological extremes result. A competitor with no empathy for his opponent is sociopathic (Mars). Rather than healthy competition, the relationship degenerates into dirty tactics and deadly violence (think terrorism). Dependent personality disorder (Venus) is a consequence of excessive loving with no trust of being loved in return, as suggested by the book title *Women Who Love Too Much*.* And a performer that cannot identify with his audience is narcissistic (Sun)—craving more and more attention, but never attending *to* the other. In short, pathology is a consequence of splitting an archetype into opposite extremes and only identifying with one side.

That side of the archetype with which one identifies is the light side. Conversely, the dark side is repressed and projected, e.g., one's Martian foe becomes a lethal enemy; one's Venusian beloved becomes pathologically jealous; or one's Solar audience becomes cruelly rejecting. Without realizing it, however, the light side becomes increasingly like the dark side in reaction to what has been projected.

If the shadow is Mars, there can be a splitting of the warrior-foe archetype such that one's enemies become extreme and one's means for survival must likewise be extreme. Yet, too much Martian assertion in defense of freedom becomes violence. If the shadow is Venus, the lover-beloved archetype is split into good lover and bad lover, betrayer and betrayed, abuser and abused. Once betrayed, however, the good lover may retaliate with abusive behavior. A Neptunian shadow derives from splitting the compassionate savior and suffering victim into opposite extremes.

---

* See Norwood, R. (1986). *Women who love too much.* Los Angeles: Jeremy Tarcher, Inc. Robin Norwood was one of the first people to describe so called "co-dependency" wherein one person tries to reform or heal another via a pathological version of love.

Too much Neptunian compassion often leads to co-dependency and resultant victimization by the victim. A Jupiter shadow entails splitting faith and doubt, or moral from immoral. Yet, too much Jupiterian faith becomes dogmatism and fanaticism—a tendency to disbelieve rival ideologies in the extreme. Jung said that ideological extremism is 'shouted down doubt'. In seeking justice, the hyper-moral person may ultimately resort to immoral measures, rationalizing that the end justifies the means.

Once possessed by the shadow, individuals will justify their extreme behavior on the basis of the extreme and insidious condition of "the other." In effect, the good that one attempts—the light side—is compensatory to the evil that one anticipates. Imagine stretching a rubber band until suddenly it snaps in two with each half pulling *away* from its counterpart. This is the condition of a ruptured archetype; each side is rigidly polarized to the other with no conscious connection to mediate the relationship. Having rejected one half of an archetype, the person retracts in the opposite direction, throwing its counterpart into shadow. The light side of the split archetype is merely an attempt to strip the planet of its negative potentialities. As such, it is extreme in the opposite direction; a flattened out, counterfeit imitation of its full-bodied self (see Figure 1, p.11). Light-side excesses are based on a perception that the opposite polarity is externally pervasive, e.g., Mars becomes stridently defensive in reaction to rampant aggression, Neptune becomes a compulsive rescuer in response to extensive tragedy, Jupiter's dogmatism is a necessary cure-all to an epidemic of godlessness, and so on.

Jung's principle of enantiodromia states that this type of imbalance cannot continue indefinitely, for the psyche always strives for balance. As Guggenbuhl-Craig asserts, "A split archetype tries persistently to return to its original polarity."[6] Eventually, each side of the archetype will become eroticized, thus assuring its eventual reunion. This is why Pluto/Scorpio is associated not only with the shadow, but also with eroticism. Nothing is so sexy as the forbidden.

Erotic energy is the means whereby fear is eradicated and wholeness restored. But the erotic is not merely sexual. Eroticism occurs in any emotionally charged relationship in which transformation is possible for both parties. Once the individual surrenders to an erotic attraction and re-establishes a connection to the dark other, the rubber band, still stretched, is likely to snap back. When it does, the individual "flip-flops" into the opposite polarity. This is called "falling into your shadow." The good cop goes bad, the prostitute converts to fundamentalism, and the priest turns lascivious.

Pluto itself constitutes its own polarity, which we can define as healer-wounded or doctor-patient. The image of the wounded healer symbolizes an acute and painful awareness of woundedness as a perennially existing counter-pole to health. Everyone has within him the health-sickness archetype. At some point in life we *will* be sick, physically or psychically. Invariably some part of the psyche will be dysfunctional, repressed, associated with pain, and feared. Ideally, the healer recognizes the potential of pain and sickness within himself, and this awareness makes him the patient's brother rather than his master. Healing has a special fascination for the healer with a true vocation. For he or she is interested in the health-sickness archetype and is fated to experience it.

According to Guggenbuhl-Craig, the primal image of the helper-healer has always been associated with power—power over life and death, and over suffering and relief of suffering. The archaic doctor was the medicine man (shaman, witch doctor, magician, sorcerer), whose power was linked to the fact that he was not only a doctor but also a priest in contact with the higher forces. The individual who was wounded, suffering, or close to death was

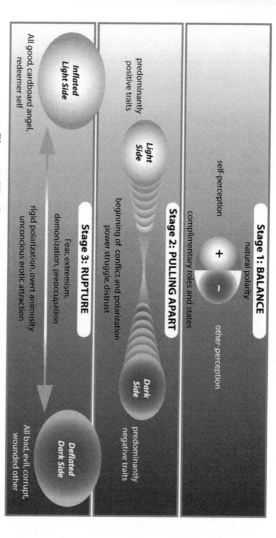

Stage 1: BALANCE

natural polarity

self-perception

complimentary roles and states

other-perception

+ −

Stage 2: PULLING APART

Light Side

predominantly positive traits

beginning of conflict and polarization
power struggle, distrust

Dark Side

predominantly negative traits

Stage 3: RUPTURE

Inflated Light Side

All good, cardboard angel, redeemer self

Fear, extremism, demonization, preoccupation

rigid polarization, overt animosity
unconcious erotic attraction

Deflated Dark Side

All bad, evil, corrupt, wounded other

Figure 1: The Devolution of a Ruptured Archetype

In **stage 1** there is no polarization. Opposites are divided into complementary roles and states, and the individual can identify with either side. Both sides are balanced, neither all good nor all bad. In **stage 2**, there is the beginning of polarization with resultant power struggle and distrust. The archetype is splitting into predominantly positive and predominantly negative traits. In **stage 3**, the rupture is complete. Opposites are rigidly polarized with each side exaggerated into black and white extremes, i.e., "all good" or "all bad" caricatures of the archetype. The relationship is characterized by intense fear, overt animosity, compulsive preoccupation, and unconscious erotic attraction.

comparatively powerless and dependent upon the medicine man. Even today when someone is dominated by fear, tortured by pain, or threatened by death, they become as children, looking for the all-powerful healer. A strange form of regression takes place. Patients become childish and submissive, looking for someone to assume the dominant roll. Great power is projected onto the doctor, who becomes almost a god-like redeemer. The doctor can heal the sick, ease pain, and make the experience of suffering bearable. A polarity takes place with the regressed, childish, fearful patient at one end, and the superior, mature, powerful physician at the other.

This same process can typify any planet to which Pluto forms a hard aspect. The shadow results from the splitting of a planetary archetype into an extreme good (healer) and an extreme bad (wounded) version. The side that is repressed (the dark) accumulates an intense charge. Like a pressure-cooker, its energy tends to be explosive when finally released. To the extent that the individual repudiates his dark side, it will be projected onto people or circumstances that appear to embody it *excessively*. While the dark side constellates the "wounded" half of the planetary archetype, the light side is imbued with healing powers and seeks out its wounded shadow half to redeem. And sooner or later the shadow will show up at one's front door, knocking loudly. For the sake of wholeness, one will eventually let it in (perhaps in a weak moment or due to a fatal fascination) and so become possessed by the repudiated instinct. This can mean compulsively falling in love with someone who is untrustworthy (Pluto-Venus), fighting a corrupt enemy (Pluto-Mars), caring for someone who is counter-dependent (Pluto-Moon), or seeking to convert an atheist (Pluto-Jupiter).

In sum, splitting the wounded-healer archetype can potentially infect all planets that Pluto aspects by hard angle. Like a lethal virus that spreads throughout the psyche, each aspected planet is abducted into the underworld and split into two halves, one extremely good, one extremely bad. The individual identifies with the light side and projects the other. Each polarity then tends to manifest in an intense, dysfunctional manner. Invariably, the dark side will appear to be wounded and in need of regeneration. In reality, however, it is the planet itself that needs to be healed.

THE ASTROLOGER'S SHADOW

I would like to return now to a point I made earlier. Why would anyone *choose* a career that is disreputable? It's one thing if the career promises fast cash in large quantities, like drug dealing, but that's hardly the case with astrology. We would all probably make more money installing sprinkler systems. What makes astrology attractive to its practitioners? I suspect that something in us must identify with astrology's outlaw status; otherwise, we would not be so powerfully drawn to it.

Because astrology is a forbidden doctrine, i.e., one not permitted in our cultures academic institutions, the very choice of astrology as a career implies that career itself is bound up with shadow issues. This suggests some kind of connection between Pluto and Saturn in the chart.* Recall the shadow tends to be what we *avoid*. If our capacity for success (Saturn) is wounded, then the choice of astrology as a career would be consistent with this condition, i.e., the cultural message of "astrology is not a legitimate profession" may mirror an intrapsychic prohibition around success. I am not saying this is the only reason that one becomes an astrologer, i.e.,

---

* While not every astrologer is going to have a hard aspect between Pluto and Saturn, there are at least twelve other ways these archetypal principles can be connected—Pluto in the 10th, Saturn in the 8th, Pluto aspecting a planet in the 10th, Saturn aspecting a planet in the 8th, Scorpio on the M.C., the ruler of the 10th in the 8th, the ruler of the 8th in the 10th, Pluto aspecting the ruler of the M.C., Saturn aspecting the ruler of the 8th, Saturn in Scorpio, Pluto in Capricorn, planets in the 10th forming a closing quincunx to other planets, or any combination of all of the above. The more connections of this sort one observes, the more likely the native's career involves shadow issues.

it is solely a neurotic impulse, but I am saying it can be a factor for some people, perhaps more than we realize.

One of the consequences of Saturn-Pluto dynamics is that one's career is likely to include a Plutonian dimension. Of course, there are healthy ways in which this can be accomplished, the most obvious being a career in the helping-healing professions. Yet, very often people end up in careers that are associated with things forbidden, dark, or risky—like astrology. Who among us hasn't suffered the embarrassment of a snide remark or a startled look when we admit that we're astrologers? Many astrologers have difficulty advancing or promoting their careers due to unconscious shame (Pluto).

A core principle in psychology is that early negative messages can contribute to grim, unconscious, pathogenic beliefs. These beliefs, in turn, underlie harmful patterns of thinking and feeling that are "acted out" unconsciously. The term "acting out" refers to the direct expression of impulses without apparent conscious reflection or regard for negative consequences. For example, if children are conditioned to believe that they are bad, they may later behave in ways that are destructive to themselves or others. Their "bad" behavior expresses an unconscious conviction that they are bad.

"Badness" (taboo) can be associated with any planet that forms a hard aspect to Pluto. Some people, for example, have an unconscious conviction that their need for success (Saturn) is bad. Let's speculate, for example, that there is something in a woman's history (in this life or a previous one) that prohibits her from succeeding in her career. Perhaps her father was a failure or felt impotent in his profession. Due to his shame, he wasn't able to support his daughter's ambitions. Or he couldn't model for her how to *be* a success. This may result in a fear that she will "out-do" him and thus contribute further to his pain. Perhaps the message was that girls are not supposed to be superior to boys. Her shadow, therefore, is bound up with issues of superior/inferior, adequate/inadequate, and success/failure—polarities that we associate with Saturn. Saturnian processes and phenomena are associated with something harmful, shameful, and forbidden (Pluto).

If the individual associates "profession" with "forbidden," she may act out by choosing a forbidden profession, e.g., a profession of ill repute that is associated with being a charlatan. Astrology fits the bill. Selection of astrology as a career may actually be an "acting out" of a Saturn wound. Fear and shame around success is expressed by unconsciously choosing a career that is culturally despised. Astrologers are striving to succeed in a field that *de facto* is considered fraudulent.

Being an astrologer also means believing in a doctrine that is taboo. This suggests that Jupiter, too, may in some way be involved with Pluto, for Jupiter symbolizes belief systems, ideologies, and philosophies.* The choice of a doctrine that has been banned from licensed and accredited professions may be an "acting out" of a Jupiter shadow. Just as one's capacity for success (Saturn) can be prohibited for unconscious reasons, so can one's capacity for faith. Let's create an imaginary scenario in which an individual has an unconscious conviction that conventional religious doctrines are false and dangerous. Perhaps in a previous life a woman was a good Christian but was wrongly accused of being a witch. She was subsequently tortured by religious authorities and burned at the stake. It is not difficult to imagine how this might contribute to a fear of orthodox religion—i.e., a prohibition against believing.

I once had a client with Jupiter in Scorpio in the 10th squaring a Saturn/Pluto conjunction in Leo in the 7th. Her father was a

---

* Just as with Saturn, there are at least twelve ways that Jupiter and Pluto can have a dialogue. Likewise, there are twelve ways that Jupiter and Saturn can be connected. For practical purposes, however, I will limit my comments mostly to hard aspects between these three planets.

religious fundamentalist and rabid Republican. If she disagreed with any of his convictions he was apt to pick up a chair and throw it at her. In effect, she was terrorized by his faith, which was *extreme.*

If fear is associated with matters of faith, one may act out by unconsciously choosing a doctrine that *is* dangerous. Again, astrology fits the bill. In several states, we actually run the risk of being arrested for professing our beliefs and practicing our craft. As a belief-system, astrology is associated with criminal behavior (Pluto). Small wonder that astrologers have difficulty advancing their careers through promotion or advertising (which are Jupiter functions). Many of us have profound misgivings about *any* kind of recognition as astrologers.

While Pluto itself symbolizes the shadow, this is even more relevant when we consider astrology as a profession. To a great extent, our role is that of helper-healers. Like physicians, we are often dealing with people that are in pain or in crisis. In effect, Pluto is implicit in the astrologer's shadow. It's the dark glue that binds together its Jupiter and Saturn components.

In sum, while there are innumerable ways that being an astrologer might show up in the chart, it would seem that some sort of connection between Saturn, Jupiter, and Pluto is implicit.* First, one's career entails a profession that is disreputable (Saturn-Pluto). Second, it requires belief in a doctrine that is forbidden (Jupiter-Pluto). And three, career itself entails helping-healing (Pluto). I submit that connections between these three archetypes are inherent in the astrologer's shadow. One is a career factor, the other is a doctrinal factor, and the last is a healer-helper factor. The astrologer's shadow would seem inescapably linked with issues of

---

* Other planets may likewise have importance for an astrological career. For example, Uranus and Neptune may each in their own way be associated with astrology. Uranus provides a holistic perspective that has an enlightening effect, and Neptune confers a spiritual understanding of the numinous, symbol-laden world of the psyche. However, for various reasons, these planets are less likely to be bound up with generic shadow issues for astrologers.

authority and wisdom as these are applied in one's profession as a helper-healer. I will now examine each of these factors in detail.

SATURN'S SHADOW

Saturn's shadow derives from splitting its natural polarities into light and dark. These polarities include governor-governed, superior-subordinate, and success-failure. In real life, we have to play *all* these roles. There are times to respect the rules and subordinate oneself to the system, and other times when we must take control and exercise authority. Likewise, sometimes we succeed, other times we fail; no one succeeds all the time and no one fails all the time. If Saturn is thrown into shadow, however, then *any* Saturn role can wax extreme due to the rigidity that results.

Hard Saturn-Pluto aspects tend to create difficulties with authority, either *as* an authority, or in relation *to* authorities. If one is in authority, he may project that his subordinates are disloyal and must be subjugated; thus, he feels compelled to devalue, reform, or eliminate his "bad" (wounded) inferiors. Saturn has fallen into shadow whenever someone tries too hard to succeed. Often there is a ruthless, corrupt, driven style. He may imagine that others are envious of his position and want to take him down. Because he is uncomfortable with his own success, he projects that others would like to see him fail. This is the person who cuts corners, breaks the rules, and seeks to destroy his "enemies," all for the sake of strengthening control. Often, this is justified as a "necessary evil" in order to reform a corrupt system.*

Needless to say, there is a tremendous potential for abuse of authority in this scenario. Unable to identify with Saturn's subordinate role, which is split off and projected onto inferiors,

---

* With Pluto in the 10th, Richard Nixon is a good example. His rise to power was largely due to his campaign against "the red menace" (communism) that he claimed was corrupting government. Ultimately, of course, it was revealed that Nixon himself was corrupt.

they do the only thing that is left—seize the reins of power and run with it, damn the consequences, use *extreme* authority. Thus Saturn's shadow is the despot, autocrat, or tyrant.

Conversely, if one is in a subordinate position, there can be paranoia that those in control are corrupt and have malevolent intentions. One is wounded by the dark, dominant other. This may start with the father and later get projected onto bosses, superiors, and the government. He or she may identify with the disempowered masses that seek to reform or overthrow those in power.* As astrologers, this can manifest as a perception that the system—science, academia—is against us, i.e., we are disempowered as a profession and must fight an uphill battle.

Equally possible, an astrologer may overidentify with being a failure and avoid taking actions that would be necessary for realistic achievement. She may feel undeserving of success, or believe that if she strives to "climb the ladder" those on top will knock her down. If she is convinced that the deck is stacked against her, then it becomes futile to try; humiliation and degradation will be her only reward. Because the likelihood of failure is increased as a consequence of attitudes that are disempowering, she becomes her own worst enemy.

I have a client with Pluto opposition Saturn who believes that if he subordinates himself to a company he'll be devoured. It will dominate him utterly and he will lose all sense of control. Thus, he avoids any actions that might actually advance his career. His projection is that all authorities (bosses, superiors) are wounded like his Dad and must have complete control. If he challenges their dictates he'll be cut off and cast adrift in a sea of perpetual failure. If he submits, he'll be dominated. In the internal story

---

* At the time of this writing, Saturn and Pluto are in opposition and a superpower—the United States—is preparing for war against an inferior power—Afghanistan and the terrorists it harbors. On a collective level, one can readily see Saturn-Pluto dynamics at work.

that he's constructed, he's damned either way since there is no room for a sharing of power or success. On the other hand, he also fears becoming an authority, as if he'll hurt others by assuming responsibility for their success. He anticipates that he will dominate them and steal *their* power. In his mind, exercise of his authority can actually be damaging to the other person.

Whether one assumes or avoids authority, the Saturn role is characterized by fear, extremism, and rigidity. The astrologer is either afraid he will *never* succeed—or, if he does, he must remain vigilant against those who would plot against him. Fulfillment of the Saturnian drive is ever threatened and vulnerable.

THE SATURN DEFLATION FACTOR

Another way that Saturn can operate as a shadow is through deflation, which is the condition of being disheartened and discouraged. Psychologically, to deflate means to reduce the importance of something or someone. When the astrologer's shadow manifests as deflation it constitutes an avoidance of success due to the shame associated with being an astrologer.

Prior to the birth of modern science, astrology enjoyed a central and honored place in virtually every culture since the dawn of humanity. Subsequent to the 17th century, however, astrology has been profoundly deflated. The status of today's astrologer has been downsized from court advisor to court fool. While the archetype of *fool* has certain positive connotations, what I mean is that contemporary astrologers are no longer taken seriously by the academic and scientific establishment. Rather, they are invited to feel silly or even ashamed of themselves.

This is not to say that people do not successfully apply astrology in diverse fields. Of course, they do. But there are risks involved. Recall the outcry when it was discovered that Nancy Reagan utilized the services of astrologer Joan Quigley in scheduling the affairs of then President Ronald Reagan. The very fact that astrology is not taught in academic institutions is testimony to its lowly status. A lack of credentialing contributes to the perception that we are frauds. Astrologers routinely give advice and perform functions that require licensure in other fields; yet, we ourselves cannot be licensed. We are tolerated in Sun sign columns for having entertainment value, but many people would regard it as scandalous if a respected scientist, doctor, or politician admitted that he actually used astrology in his work.

Because astrology is not officially endorsed by western culture, we constitute a kind of out-group—a lowly caste of inferior beings that are tolerated but not respected. How difficult is it then for us to respect ourselves? There are almost no degrees or licenses in astrology that can confirm our competence as professionals.* The absence of such credentials evidences astrology's status as a non-profession. In effect, astrology has been driven underground. This is why it is a shadow profession.

In the late 90's The Astrological Institute in Phoenix was granted accreditation as a trade school by the federal Accrediting Commission of Career Schools and Colleges. This was great news for astrologers. The Astrological Institute is the first accredited trade school in our field. Predictably, however, this precipitated an attack by scientific "experts". Neil Tyson, an astrophysicist who heads the Hayden Planetarium in New York, asserts that astrology was discredited 600 years ago with the birth of modern science:

> To teach it as though you are contributing to the fundamental knowledge of an informed electorate is astonishing in this, the 21st century. Education should be about knowing how to think, and part of knowing how to think is knowing how

---

* Bath College in England and The Academy of AstroDPsychology in Haddam Neck, CT are helping to rectify this situation.

the laws of nature shape the world around us. Without that knowledge, without that capacity to think, you can easily become a victim of people who seek to take advantage of you.*

This kind of comment is typical of the scientific intelligentsia. The implication is that astrology is not a valid career and that astrologers are frauds who victimize innocent people.

THE IMPOSTER SYNDROME

Deflation is consistent with what psychologists call *the imposter syndrome.*[7] Individuals with imposter syndrome suffer vague feelings of self-doubt, angst and intellectual fraudulence despite outward signs of competence. External proof of intelligence and ability in the form of academic excellence, degrees, recognition, promotions and the like are routinely dismissed. Instead, success is attributed to contacts, luck, timing, perseverance, personality, or having "fooled" others into thinking they were smarter and more capable than they "knew" themselves to be. Rather than offering assurance, each new achievement and subsequent challenge only serves to intensify the ever-present fear of being found out as an "imposter."

There is a high likelihood for astrologers to suffer from imposter syndrome for the simple reason that they are *de facto* considered fraudulent. If you suffer from imposter syndrome, you're likely to fear success as much as you do failure. It's a double-bind that seems to reflect a splitting of the Saturn archetype. If someone with imposter syndrome makes a mistake, they interpret it as proof of their imposter status. Thus errors cannot be utilized as opportunities for learning or improvement; rather, there is likely to be a frantic "cover-up" that entails elaborate defenses that shift the

---

* Reported in The Philadelphia Inquirer, U.S. & World, "Astrology school in Arizona wins federal accreditation," August 28, 2001.

blame to someone else. On the other hand, success brings it's own problems, for now their accomplishments may bring additional exposure and new tests of competence. Success merely amplifies the fear of being "found out".

With imposter syndrome, Saturn is stretched to extremes on each side. Both failure and success evoke such fear that astrologers cannot benefit from either. Situations in which their competence might be "tested" (a favorite Saturn word) are avoided. Again, the problem is not actual incompetence; it's an irrational fear of incompetence reinforced by a culture that denigrates the very subject they profess to know something about.

Saturnian processes of procrastination and perfectionism are favorite strategies to avoid being "found out". Astrologers may spend endless hours studying and taking classes without ever feeling "ready" to launch their careers. Some may do the occasional "reading" but avoid taking steps necessary for full success. Because their mastery of the subject is imperfect, they will procrastinate in key areas such as creating business cards, brochures, or a web site. Similarly, there is a reluctance to promote oneself through public speaking, writing books and articles, teaching classes, or networking in general—anything that might put them in the public eye and signal, "I'm an astrologer."

All of this is evidence of a Saturn shadow. The fear of success/failure is so intensely charged that the astrologer will actually avoid doing anything in which her competence will be tested. Unconsciously, there is an expectation of humiliation. The very choice of astrology as a career expresses fear of Saturn functions. The person does not admit this fear consciously; they don't go around saying, "I'm afraid I don't have the right stuff...I'm a failure...I'm not competent." Instead, these negative potentialities are relegated to Saturn's dark side and embodied in the shadow.

As stated, one of the primary ways in which the shadow

manifests is through projection, and this can involve both negative and positive polarities. On the negative side, the shadow fuels animosity toward figures that embody one's negative potentials. These may be other astrologers that are perceived as incompetent, poorly trained, or untrustworthy. I suspect this is why there is so much bickering and internecine battles within the field of astrology. Many of us are perpetrators or recipients of negative Saturn projections. It doesn't help, of course, that many of us *are* poorly trained due to not being able to study astrology in our culture's academic institutions. Without a means to demonstrate competency via credentialing, we turn against ourselves.

INFLATION & THE GOD COMPLEX

Compensatory to the shadow is the ideal self, or what Jung called the *persona* (Latin for *mask*). This is the positive polarity of the shadow, the light side. The ideal self is a composite of personal characteristics and potentialities that the individual believes is necessary for success, prestige, and external validation. Just as negative qualities can be projected onto suitable carriers, so positive qualities can be projected as well. If the astrologer's shadow is a mixture of negative Jupiter-Saturn qualities, the ideal self is a composite of positive Jupiter-Saturn traits. These may be projected onto figures that the individual perceives to be extraordinarily wise and successful in the field of astrology. To the extent that the shadow remains unconscious, however, one's idealizing projections become increasingly positive—to the point of being *extreme*. It is not the balanced, credible, or grounded astrologer that draws the projection, but the one that is inflated, grandiose, and omniscient—in other words, one with a God-complex.

The light side of the psyche always compensates its dark side. If deflation involves a reduction in self-importance, then inflation entails its enlargement. My thesis is that the astrologer's shadow involves negative Saturn-Jupiter-Pluto characteristics—a fear of failure, ignorance, and powerlessness. In an effort to distance from one's fears, the astrologer identifies with their opposite: an abundance of super-positive Saturn-Jupiter-Pluto traits. These might be summarized as "perfect healing wisdom."

The compensatory, inflated version of our shadow is the all-knowing, supremely wise consultant. Astrologers suffering from inflation seem to have no apparent limitations on what they can know about their client's past, present, or future. They write books, give lectures, and make claims of transcendental knowledge. Dogmatic pronouncements gush from their mouths without any evidential basis. Speculation masquerades as revelation. Instead of critical thinking, we get creative fiction. Something that *could* be true is alleged as *actually* true, with no discernable appreciation of the difference. After revealing details about your past lives, the inflated astrologer will tell you why you are the way you are now, how you should be, what profession you should be in, where you should live, and who you should marry. And, most disturbing of all, they have their followers—zombie like automatons entranced with their guru's every utterance.

If we deconstruct this inflationary composite, we find it consists of a number of interrelated parts, all of which represent split halves of whole archetypes. In the case of Pluto-Saturn dynamics, this entails splitting success from failure, superior from inferior, and authority from subordination. When the "positive" side of Saturn is carried to an extreme, the person seems possessed by a need for success. He is driven, overfunctioning, and obsessed with control. A workaholic, he feels continually pressured to measure up to unrelentingly high standards. A pretense of superiority masks a deeper, hidden, inferiority complex. This highly anxious, overachiever must prove himself superior to compensate for a fear of failure. In effect, Saturn's shadow side—failure, inadequacy, and lack of authority—is so terrifying that the entire personality is organized against it.

If Saturn is aspecting Jupiter, then the arena of overachievement might include consulting, teaching, or publishing. Integration between these two planets can produce significant accomplishment in the aforementioned areas. If, however, Saturn forms a hard aspect to Jupiter and is *not* well integrated, then the fear of failure may extend to the Jupiterian realm.* Astrologers may worry that their wisdom is scant, their faith lacking, and their capacity to discern the truth limited by lack of education or training. Their ability to perform Jupiter functions is cast into doubt. The result may be a compensatory need to produce definite, indubitable truths. Rather than admit one's feelings of inadequacy in the realm of higher knowledge, the person reacts in the opposite direction: s/he becomes the supremely wise consultant.

The problem is compounded when Jupiter is under stress from Pluto. On the up side, Jupiter-Pluto contacts can be associated with occult philosophy, which strives to explain supernatural influences, agencies, and phenomena. Astrology is a branch of occult philosophy in that it purports to explain the synchronicities between psyche and cosmos—a supernatural phenomenon. Likewise, the person might be attracted to theories that purport to explain the mysteries of death and rebirth. Astrology is strongly wedded to the doctrine of reincarnation. Since Pluto has to do with power and Jupiter with advice, aspects between Jupiter and Pluto might entail the dispensing of powerful advice. Astrologers have traditionally wielded great power. Their sage advice could influence kings by providing information on a variety of important matters—the outbreak of wars, disease, or famine, the state of the king's finances, alliances, and other critical (Pluto) issues.

---

* Once again, there are many ways that Jupiter and Saturn can be connected in addition to hard aspects, e.g., the ruler of the 10th in the 9th, Saturn in the 9th, Jupiter in the 10th, the ruler of the 9th in the 10th, and so on.

However, if Jupiter and Pluto are not integrated, then one's capacity for faith can be wounded and one's belief system bound up with shadowy doctrines. With Jupiter abducted into the underworld of the psyche, the individual is predisposed to believe that the truth has been covered-up and that it's exposure could be dangerous. The natural polarities of Jupiter—true-false, right-wrong, good-bad, wise-foolish, and faith-doubt—are torn into opposite halves with the light side inflated and the dark side projected.

The shadow side of Jupiter-Pluto entails a fear that one's truth claims could be wrong. Merely having an opinion may feel risky, as if it could harm the other and evoke a retaliatory response. One may also harbor doubts about the reality of a higher intelligence (a divine Mind) that transcends one's own. Life becomes meaningless to this exact degree, and if life is meaningless, how can one counsel others and help them to see the meaning of their experience?

Since all of this is profoundly unsettling, the astrologer may substitute inflation to compensate for deflation. This entails denying one's potential for wrongness/doubt and exaggerating the opposite polarity. The inflated astrologer is always right and never wrong, has an answer for every question, is an inspiring beacon of faith, and evidences a fervent desire to convert nonbelievers. In effect, they become "closed systems" trapped in an ideology that is fiercely defended due to the fear that it could be *wrong*. Their thinking becomes rigid, ingrown, and increasingly paranoid.

One of the consequences of Jupiter inflation is that astrologers will unconsciously fear their clients. The client's condition of wounded faith is precisely what the astrologer represses and projects. It is a general rule of Pluto that whatever we project has power, for if we open ourselves to it we may be irrevocably changed. Accordingly, astrologers with Jupiter-Pluto contacts who are wounded in their capacity to believe are apt to subjugate clients with dogmatic pronouncements of absolute knowledge.

This may be expressed via interpretations that purport to expose critical areas of life concern, e.g., "You were brutally raped in a prior life and that's why you avoid intimacy today," or "Next year you will meet your soul mate, *trust* me." Note, however, that such claims can neither be confirmed nor disconfirmed; their felt importance, however, keeps the client coming back for more. The astrologer's interpretations have an alluring, addictive quality, like a drug. All of this, I submit, is compensatory to hidden doubts about the veracity of one's knowledge claims.

JUPITER'S DARK SIDE: THE FALSE PROPHET

Under ideal circumstances, the astrologer is mid-wife to the gods; he reads the stars and translates their import in human affairs. His clients rightfully expect him to be a humble servant of the divine will. However, the dark side of this noble image is the lying hypocrite who uses astrology not because he believes but in order to gain influence and power. This may not be his conscious motive, of course, for that is the nature of the shadow; it influences us from the unconscious.

Since we cannot prove what we claim to know, we are expected to provide by our own behavior a foundation for the trust that we hope to inspire.* We want potential clients to have *faith* in astrology. Yet, this opens the door to the false prophet—the wish to present oneself to the world (and to oneself) as wiser and more knowing than we really are. With Jupiter-Pluto aspects, we may forget that doubt is the companion of faith. Even Christ on the

---

* Proof of astrological claims is notoriously difficult, not because astrology lacks validity, but because the nature of our system does not readily conform to the strictures of the experimental method. There are few astrological claims that can be statistically proven in the empirical sense. Non-experimental, qualitative methods are better suited to astrological research, but these methods are not oriented toward "proof".

cross was reputed to have said, "Father, Father, why hast thou forsaken me?" No one has perfect, undeviating faith. Likewise, no human being is omniscient. Yet, astrologers are expected to know everything—what career the client should have, who the client should marry, where the client should live, what the client did in a past life, what's going to happen next, and so on. No other profession on earth is burdened with such expectations.

Very often it is the astrologer's clients who involuntarily activate his dark brother. As interpreters of celestial intelligences that transcend the human realm, we speak with the authority of the cosmos. To the extent that we do this well, clients endow us with tremendous power (Pluto). They want us to know everything about their past, their present, and their future. No one wishes to hear the astrologer say, "I don't know," or, "I'm not sure if this is right," or "I simply don't know how to advise you in this matter." Thus the astrologer may be seduced into being the false prophet by striving to meet his client's expectations even when these expectations are grossly unrealistic. He elevates himself with high-flown words in order to hide his doubts and mask a discomforting uncertainty.

When doing consultations, astrologers often deal with intractable problems of fate, vague complaints, psychosomatic ailments, thorny dilemmas, and tragic destinies for which there are no simple answers, and very often no answers at all. Often we don't know if we are helping, or even whether the patient can be helped. Are we capable of admitting these doubts? Or do we suppress them and keep the lid on tight?

As counselors, we work with hunches and intuitions. Concepts and theories are the tools of our trade. Yet, there is great pressure to represent these tools as better than they really are and thus become the victim of the astrologer's shadow. By pretending to know the answer to every question, the astrologer acts like a little god whose knowledge encompasses the entire expanse of time and space. There is the grandiose presumption that everything on earth can be explained by something in the chart—a lunar node, a transit, solar arc, fixed star, midpoint, asteroid, Arabic part, or a transneptunian planet (when in doubt, just *make up* a planet). It is easy to forget that the interpretations we provide are products of a highly subjective, ultimately creative act. There are no givens in the realm of astrology, only constructions.

The astrologer is not likely to be told by her clients that she is inflated. In fact, clients will encourage the false prophet in the astrologer to the extent that they project their own Jupiter. If clients suffer a lack of faith in a higher power, they are more likely to turn to an oracle for guidance and hope. "Please, what do the gods have in store for me? Why did this happen? What should I do?" So long as the astrologer keeps providing answers, the questions will keep coming, and the accolades, and the projections.

The astrologer may have the impression that her work is going splendidly the deeper she falls into her shadow. Increasingly, relationships with clients are characterized by a *folie a deux*, or "double insanity." This can be defined as an unconscious collusion in which the client and the astrologer both agree that the client knows nothing and the astrologer knows everything. The client goes comatose and the astrologer grows grandiose!

THE CHARLATAN AND THE HYPOCHONDRIAC

If Saturn's shadow is the tyrant and Jupiter's is the false prophet, Pluto's dark side is the charlatan. The charlatan, or quack, is the imposter syndrome made real; it is a person who makes elaborate, fraudulent claims to skill or knowledge, often of a medical or therapeutic nature. The Charlatan's objective is less to help the client and more to help himself, financially and in terms of prestige. At best, says Guggenbuhl-Craig (1991), the charlatan "deceives himself along with his patients—at worst, deceives only his patients."[8]

Like the shadow of Jupiter and Saturn, Pluto's dark side is a consequence of splitting a whole archetype into opposite halves. Pluto's natural polarities are doctor-patient, health-sickness, and power-powerlessness. It must be remembered, however, that physician and patient are two aspects of the same archetype. For either to be effective, the one has to contain the other in awareness. Pluto is both the wound to be healed and the healer of the wound; in effect, Pluto is the wounded-healer.*

When a person becomes sick, the wounded-healer archetype is constellated. A sick person will seek an outer healer while at the same time activating his inner healer. Physicians refer to this intrapsychic healer as the "healing factor" in the patient; it is the physician *within*. To the extent that patients have the courage and willingness to confront their own illness, their recovery is facilitated. I am reminded of Dylan Thomas' poem to his dying father.

> *Do not go gentle into that good night...*
> *Rage, rage, against the dying of the light.*

Doctors recognize that the healing factor is independent of any actual medical treatment. Without the curative action of the inner healer, neither wounds nor neuroses can heal. We can stitch up a wound or provide ongoing psychotherapy, but something in the patient's body and psyche must help if an ailment is to be overcome.

Just as the patient must access his inner physician, so the doctor must be in touch with her inner patient. Only by identifying

---

* I realize it has become fashionable to attribute the archetype of the wounded-healer to Chiron. Frankly, I'm not sure *what* Chiron is. There has been conflicting testimony with regard to its meaning and astronomical status—asteroid, planetoid, comet? Perhaps it constitutes a different kind of wound than Pluto, or perhaps it's merely misnamed. Mythological names for celestial objects do not always correlate with their astrological properties.

with the patient's plight can the doctor arouse the healing factor within the patient. This is especially true in psychotherapy. Jung repeatedly maintained that the analytical process must be a mutual one, with analyst and patient each effecting the other. The true wounded healer realizes that his patients are constantly mirroring him, i.e., their problems constellate his own problems, and vice versa. Thus he openly works not only on the patient, but also on himself. Paradoxically, his healing powers are strengthened by his capacity to acknowledge his own wounds.

In effect, facing one's shadow enables one to be a healing force in the lives of others. Once we integrate our dark side, we are empowered to "go in where angels fear to tread" and help the client in precisely those areas where we ourselves have been wounded. Otherwise, the individual will identify exclusively with one side and project the other. For example, a person may experience himself *only* as the all-powerful healer looking for someone who is wounded—or, as the perennially wounded patient constantly seeking a powerful healer.

The hypochondriac and the all-powerful healer are shadows of one another. When either of these roles—healer or patient—becomes frozen such that the person habitually identifies with one side but not the other, there is a splitting of the Pluto archetype. The patient projects all healing power onto the physician and becomes stuck in the patient role—helpless, childlike, and impotent. Conversely, the physician projects his wounds onto the patient and becomes stuck in the role of the omnipotent, all-knowing healer. To the extent that one's healing powers are exaggerated, one becomes the charlatan—pretentious and inflated.

Because astrologers perform a helping-healing function, they, too, are vulnerable to charlatanism. Very often the astrologer's clients are suffering from the same issues that constitute the astrologer's shadow—lack of control and fear of failure (Saturn), combined with insufficient faith and hope (Jupiter). Clients want sage advice on how to succeed in their various endeavors. And they want positive, hopeful predictions that will relieve their anxiety about an uncertain future. In meeting these needs, however, the astrologer risks falling prey to his shadow. He may begin to have the impression that lack of control and fear of the future have nothing to do with him. He feels himself to be the all-knowing oracle; he's "on top" of the future; the only wounds are those of his clients, while he is secure against them.

When an astrologer projects his woundedness onto clients and identifies exclusively with the healer pole, then his clients will leave him no peace. Their pain and fears will haunt him; he will obsess about them in fervent hope of relieving their distress. Yet, by projecting his weakness, the astrologer elevates himself at the client's expense. He becomes powerful through psychological failure rather than through strength.

To the extent that the wounded pole of Pluto is projected, the healer will seek to reunify the split archetype through power *over* the patient. In astrology, this occurs by offering a variety of pseudo-solutions to the client's problems—e.g., telling them what to do (quick-fixes), claiming their problems originate in a past life (often shaming the client), or providing reassuring but useless predictions. I suspect that the purpose of such interpretations is less to help the client and more to relieve the astrologer's anxiety about issues that he is unwilling to face in himself. If his anxiety is sufficiently high, the astrologer may actually be contemptuous of the people he is pledged to help. A good example here is the radio shrink, Dr. Laura Schlessinger, who often berates and scolds her callers with caustic advice. In such instances, the healer promotes himself while degrading the patient.*

---

* As we shall see in Chapter 2, Schlessinger's own chart has a plethora of shadow aspects of the sort described in this article, e.g., Jupiter in Scorpio and Saturn conjunct Pluto. In some ways, her story is a cautionary tale for astrologers.

Similarly, the client who represses her inner healer and projects it onto the astrologer will strive to reunify the archetype through subjection and childish dependence. Yet, she will frequently be dissatisfied with the "help" she evokes, for unconsciously she holds the healer in contempt as well. Such clients are persistently desperate yet unwilling to benefit from the help they receive. Psychotherapists call this "resistance." No one is more powerful than a patient who refuses to heal, for she will defeat the healer every time.

In sum, the splitting of Pluto—the wounded healer archetype—results in each side secretly resenting and distrusting the other. At the same time, they cannot exist without one another. The desire for power and the client's state of subjugation are both expressions of an attempt to reunify the split archetype. Yet, this kind of "help" actually addicts the client to the astrologer's pronouncements and is damaging to both healer and wounded. The wounded person becomes perennially wounded; the healer becomes perpetually inflated.

Many clients seek out psychics and astrologers in order to externalize responsibility for their lives, "Tell me what to do. What's going to happen next?" By indulging these kinds of requests, the astrologer actually conspires in keeping the client disempowered and dependent, while she herself remains a self-important, pretentious "oracle" blind to her own wounds, flaws, and limitations.

WRESTLING WITH MY SHADOW

At the beginning of this article, I posed the question, "Why did I decide to become an astrologer?" My thesis is that choice of astrology as a career may be symptomatic of psychological issues and wounds, especially as these relate to contacts between Pluto, Saturn, and Jupiter. Of course, the shadow can show up in a variety of ways—8th house planets, closing quincunxes, and a host of other configurations. Ultimately, as with any astrological question, one needs to look at the whole chart. In my own case (see Figure 2, page 36), I'd like to focus on the relationship between my Sun, Moon, and Jupiter. As we shall see, these planets eventually tie into Saturn and Pluto.

To explain the origins of my shadow, I must reveal a bit of personal history. My childhood was relatively idyllic were it not for one factor, my mother was alcoholic. Seeking to escape her dark influence, I over identified with my father. Up until my twenties, I didn't know where I began and he left off. Lack of a clearly differentiated self is certainly one way that Sun square Neptune can manifest. However, with the Sun as dispositor of my two 4th house planets (Venus and Pluto), *and* being in Cancer, I was also closely identified with the maternal principle. My mother's alcoholism (Sun square Neptune again) reflected a wound to my own identity.

This aspect is also implicated in the process of denial that was pervasive in my family. The Sun symbolizes our faculty of perception. To perceive is to create (Sun). With its square to Neptune, I was invited to distrust my perception and create an illusionary reality that all was well. Neither my father nor sister was willing to acknowledge my mother's alcoholism. Yet whenever my mother was drunk, it was impossible for me *not* to say something. "You're drunk!" I would blurt out at the dinner table, hoping someone would support my perception. My father and sister merely stared at their food while my mother launched a counter-attack. She accused me of making up lies and would act deeply hurt as if I had said something that was viciously cruel. It was crazy making. *I* was the bad one who had hurt *her*. My father and sister's silence only seemed to confirm this verdict.

Since I had feelings about my mother's alcoholism, the message to my Moon was, "You're feelings don't count; they are not to be trusted. You are wrong and bad for what you feel." Needless to say, this only exacerbated my anger and my pain. Eventually, I came to expect that this is how everyone behaved. My failure to obtain understanding or caring from my mother (at least around this painful issue) crystallized into a fear that I couldn't obtain it from *anyone*. At first sign, therefore, that my feelings and perceptions are not accepted, my impulse is to react with anger. Too often, however, this involves jumping the gun—an *over*reaction to *perceived* rejection.

How this is reflected in my chart is probably obvious. As mentioned, my Sun is squaring Neptune, which equates to experiences that involve denial of reality. More specifically, it symbolizes a denial of *my* reality—of *me*. Part of my shadow, therefore, is comprised of "deceit and denial," qualities that my mother and family embodied and which I came to project as *not-me*. These were traits that I abhorred and to which I polarized with a vengeance that clearly derived from experiences in my family.

The Moon's placement in the 8th house would seem to reflect my experience of a mother that was wounded and acting out her pain by getting drunk. Eighth house planets symbolize parts of the psyche that need to be transformed. Accordingly, they are often associated with something forbidden and imbued with pain and fear. This would correlate to not being able to trust my mother/family for containment of my feelings. During much of my early life it felt dangerous to disclose my dependency needs. Another part of my shadow, therefore, has to do with issues of emotional vulnerability. This is what I wanted to push *away* and project onto other people.

Sagittarius on the cusp of the 8th suggests that the religious impulse—the search for meaning—is also associated with danger and taboo. The Moon's placement in Sagittarius is interesting in light of the fact that my mother was an apparent atheist. I say

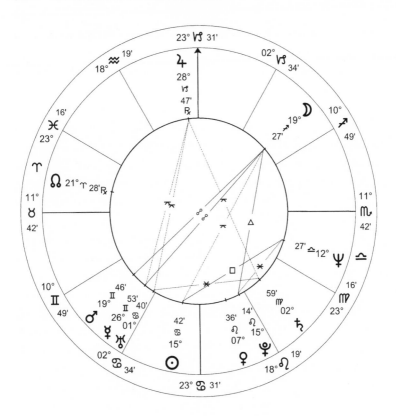

Figure 2: Glenn Perry, July 8, 1949, 1:31am, Bridgeport, CT

"apparent," because she was not an avowed atheist, yet she never went to church and struggled openly with religious doubts. The Moon's sign position symbolizes a key theme of our emotional life; it suggests what we have feelings *about*. Sagittarius, of course, has to do with matters of faith, honesty, truth, and morality—qualities that were at the heart of my mother's failure. I equated her lack of honesty with lack of caring. If I project that others, too, will be emotionally dishonest and immoral, then I may react to this perception by exaggerating my *own* caring, morality, and truthfulness. Of course, this is how the shadow forms—by identifying with qualities that are the opposite of what we project.

Since the Moon is in the 8th (Pluto's house), it falls into the house of shadows and is apt to be split into a light side and a dark side. The Moon's natural polarity is mother-child, or caregiver-care receiver. Sagittarius' polarity is that of honest-dishonest, faith-doubt, and true-false. Accordingly, if Moon Sagittarius is split into opposite halves, the light side is emotionally honest, faithful, caring, and wise, whereas the dark side is emotionally dishonest, faithless, uncaring, and unwise. Again, it would be natural for me to identify with the light side and project the dark.

The Moon's opposition to Mars also implicates the warrior archetype. What always galled me about my family was their lack of emotional courage; they seemed unwilling to face the truth. Also, there was an egocentric, selfish disregard for feelings implicit in my mother's behavior that is consistent with an unintegrated Moon-Mars opposition. I always felt that underneath her alcoholism was suppressed rage, which she acted out by drinking. Her refusal to stay sober was passive-aggressive; at least that's how I took it. While this planetary configuration has many layers of meaning, suffice to say that my family role was that of "confronter". I would angrily challenge (in typical Mars fashion) my mother's refusal to admit the truth, which I associated with lack of caring. Over time, this became an inbred, automatic pattern of response that extended beyond my family. Whenever my emotions were triggered by analogous events, I became combative and confrontive.

In short, the essence of my shadow is symbolized by Moon in Sagittarius in the 8th house opposed Mars. This entails (1) denial of feelings and hostile defensiveness; (2) selfish insensitivity to other's feelings; and (3) rejection of the need for dependence on a higher power. Of course, I didn't see myself this way; this is how I perceived others to be, especially those on whom I depended.

Recall that the shadow signifies potentialities that one cannot see or accept in oneself. Yet, the insidious thing about the shadow is that the more one reacts to what is projected, the more one's behavior becomes like the projected traits. The fact was, I didn't know how to talk about feelings either.

To the extent that I projected my wounded Moon, I polarized in the other direction by inflating my capacity to care and speak the truth. This set the stage for falling into my shadow. If I can't trust that others are emotionally real, it will be difficult for me to be emotionally real with them. If I can't have compassion for the defenses and wounds of others, or even merely for their different opinions, then I am liable to attack them as bad and wrong in the same way that my mother attacked me. In effect, I become the thing that was wounding. To become conscious of my dark side, therefore, requires recognizing that I have the potential to treat others with the same hostile defensiveness and insensitivity that I experienced as a child.

Back in my early twenties, I remember telling a fellow student that I was excited about being an astrologer because it gave me the opportunity to confront people who might be lying about the truth of what's going on *inside*. That, in effect, was my mission. Unconsciously, I wanted to work out with my clients unfinished business with my mother. Little did I realize, however, that my choice of astrology for a career entailed embracing a belief system whose rejection paralleled my own family experience. As I came increasingly to appreciate astrology's validity, its dismissal by the larger culture resonated with something deep inside. I knew what it was like to have one's feelings invalidated and one's truth attacked. On an unconscious level, I'm sure I was saying: *This time they won't get away with it.*

The ultimate manifestation of my shadow would emerge through the Moon's dispositor, Jupiter, which is in Capricorn and conjunct my M.C. With Sagittarius on the cusp of the 8th, Jupiter signifies Pluto's house. Also, with Moon in Sagittarius in the 8th, Jupiter disposits the Moon, which means that the Moon triggers Jupiter's functions. Clearly, Jupiter comes from the 8th house and is thus closely bound with Pluto's realm. The upshot of this is that emotionally wounding experiences within my family of origin constitute the motivational foundation, the ultimate catalyst, for what I am compelled to achieve in my career (10th house).

In effect, Jupiter's behavior is an extension of my lunar shadow. I am not simply motivated to develop the perfect theory (Jupiter in Capricorn), but to redress a grievance—namely, that my need to belong and to be loved was injured by a moral and religious crisis that occurred in my family of origin (Moon in Sagittarius in the 8th). My forbidden truth was acknowledgment of my mother's alcoholism and the devastating impact it had on our family. Because her emotional pain was denied, and with it the truth of her alcoholism, it was not permissible for anyone to talk about feelings (Moon). There was so much shame and embarrassment associated with her condition that we simply buried it. But like any planet in the 8th, it does not go away; it simply festers and gathers steam, looking for a way out of the underworld.

Since the Moon is in Sagittarius, the way out is Jupiter. Jupiter in the 10th inherited the legacy of a distraught Moon. Jupiter must *do* something for the Moon; thus, it appropriates a forbidden truth—astrology—and promotes it with an intensity fueled by the denial of truth in my family. On a psychological and emotional level, they are inseparably linked. I feel passionate about the theory of astrology precisely because I identify with its suppression. Just as the truth and pain of my mother's alcoholism had to be denied, so as a member of this culture I am invited to deny the truth of astrology. In effect, my astrological career serves as the vehicle for healing my shadow. I must find a way to deal with the suppression of astrology in a manner that is different from how I handled the suppression of truth in my family.

Again, the danger is my shadow. It is precisely because of the pain around my Sagittarian Moon that I find it difficult to balance faith with doubt. Just as I sought to reform my mother, so I am compelled to reform the public's perception of astrology. Zealotry, however, is the mark of an inflamed, inflated Jupiter. To act out my pain merely requires that I project onto the culture that they refuse to see the truth of what *I* know. *Their refusal to embrace astrology has consequences for the entire community*, so I tell myself.

> *It bespeaks a lack of caring, an insensitivity to astrology's importance for the helping professions. Given astrology's potential as a counseling tool, how could they not teach it in our universities? If they cared, they would admit its truth!*

This is the dialogue that goes on inside me. Such thoughts and feelings are obviously an extension of my family experience. Yet, the more I combat attacks against astrology, the more I am apt to blind myself to legitimate criticisms. Here again the shadow is at work; faith and doubt polarize into opposite extremes. Am I always right and they always wrong? Can I admit a degree of uncertainty about my own knowledge claims? As an astrologer, I may justly defend the validity of astrology, but that doesn't mean that *everything* I say is right or true.

Not only does Jupiter signify Pluto's house, but the fact that the ruler of the 8th is *in* the 10th also establishes a Saturn-Pluto connection. Sagittarian issues that need to be healed are worked out through career; thus, career is associated with woundedness and healing (no surprise there—I'm a psychotherapist). Jupiter's placement in Capricorn in the 10th house, its quincunx to Saturn, and Saturn's signification of the 9th house, all clearly show that Jupiter and Saturn are entwined as well. Thus the full array of components for the astrologer's shadow is in my chart; Jupiter, Saturn, and Pluto are in dialogue.

Jupiter's involvement with Saturn symbolizes my conviction that I can never know enough. I spent twelve years in graduate school getting my M.A. and Ph.D. Still I suffer from an imposter complex—a subtle but insidious fear that I could be exposed as a fraud, especially in the field of psychology wherein my advocacy of astrology marks me as untrustworthy. Jupiter-Saturn drives me to overcompensate. By any definition I'm a workaholic. I feel compelled to construct a theoretical edifice that is incontrovertible—a rock solid, unassailable bulwark against the black tide of disbelief that threatens to engulf our field (and my beliefs). Yet, I suspect that my perfectionism is merely procrastination in disguise. It took me more than thirty years in the field to formally publish my first book.

Suffice to say that shadow work is not easy. Although my commitment to personal growth has gradually weakened my shadow, it has merely turned it from black to gray. By no means am I out of the woods. I struggle with a tendency to be dogmatic and combative with my colleagues, and I still get incensed at public attacks against astrology. My abhorrence of astrological charlatans and false prophets may belie my own tendencies in this regard. I suspect that I compensate for a fear of meaninglessness by striving to produce certain, indubitable truths. But do I know as much as I think I do? Am I trying to present myself as wiser than I really am?

I take some solace in knowing that so long as I keep asking these questions I will keep my shadow at bay—perhaps even befriend it. I am especially grateful for what I learned in graduate school with regard to research methodology, epistemology, and critical thinking. For these courses taught me that a healthy skepticism is just as important as a strong faith. To admit what I don't know balances what I think I do know and keeps my knowledge claims from becoming inflated.

Summary and Conclusion

The shadow constitutes certain negative psychic potentialities that an individual repudiates. By exaggerating traits that are believed to be antithetical to the shadow, the psyche compensates its dark side. Thus a given archetype can be split into light and dark halves. Once the dark side is banished from consciousness, it tends to be projected onto people that appear to embody it. There is a tendency to attack or attempt to reform people that represent one's shadow.

While there is no single factor in astrology that signifies the shadow, it has much in common with Pluto. As lord of the underworld, Pluto is naturally associated with things dark and shadowy. Pluto symbolizes the wounded-healer, which necessarily has two poles: wounded and healer. When Pluto forms a hard aspect to another planet, that planet's functions tend to be split into opposite halves and mixed with the wounded-healer archetype. The planet's light and dark sides become rigidly polarized with each being expressed in an extreme way. The dark, projected side appears to be wounded, while the light, identified side feels imbued with healing potential. Because a split archetype tries persistently to return to its original polarity, the individual becomes obsessed with transforming or destroying whatever has been projected. In effect, the planet is injured and requires healing if wholeness is to be restored.

The choice to become a professional astrologer may be motivated in part by psychological wounds encapsulated in one's shadow. While the astrologer's shadow can be constellated in many ways, its most generic features seem to be comprised of Jupiter, Saturn, and Pluto dynamics. Pluto's natural polarity of healer-patient is the critical factor, which, in turn, combines with Saturnian polarities of success-failure and Jupiterian issues of faith-doubt. Once these polarities become split, the astrologer is prone to acting out in a variety of ways. If he identifies with the dark side, then feelings of failure (Saturn), ignorance (Jupiter), and impotence (Pluto) cause deflation and a fear of being exposed as an imposter. One may then avoid taking actions that enhance one's career.

Equally possible, the astrologer could overcompensate by identifying with the opposite characteristics—the light side. Inflation of Saturn-Jupiter-Pluto traits entails posturing as the all-powerful, supremely wise consultant. Variations on this theme include the tyrant, the false prophet, and the charlatan. Such roles are actually damaging to astrologer and client alike. The client is disempowered and seduced into a state of abject dependency, while the astrologer remains blind to her own weaknesses, fears, and limitations. Neither astrologer nor client is able to grow toward wholeness; thus, the process of psychological development is derailed.

The most important factor in healing one's shadow is awareness of its existence. Astrology can be an objective aid in this regard. Additionally, individuals are encouraged to notice any extremes of thinking or feeling that might characterize their actions, for extremism is the shadow's *leitmotif*. The thing that we most detest points to our shadow. Righteous indignation, shame, power struggles, chronic resentment, hatefulness, malevolent intentions, and vindictiveness are all red flags.

It is important to realize that such feelings are not necessarily indicative of one's own culpability, e.g., my abhorrence of false prophets does not mean I *am* a false prophet. What it indicates is a *fear* of false prophesying within myself. I may, in fact, evidence no false prophet tendencies; I may even go to the opposite extreme. Yet, it is my inability to allow for the potential of false prophet behavior—inflated claims, hypocrisy, pretensions of omniscience— that generates my shadow.

The key to shadow work is to recognize, like the poet Terence, "nothing that is human is foreign to me." There is a story about an English judge who looks deeply into a murderer's eyes and recognizes the killing impulse in his own soul. After condemning the man to death, the judge utters the immortal words, "There but for the grace of God go I."

The solution to the shadow is not putting a white light around everything that is awful in the world. The thing that we abhor may, in fact, be deserving of our enmity. There *is* authentic evil that needs to be eradicated. People *do* bad things; there are wrongs that need to be righted. The important thing is to admit, like the English judge, that we have the potential to do what we would not do—and, when we do the wrong thing, to forgive oneself for not measuring up to an ideal, for not being perfect. Shadow work for astrologers especially means having the courage to admit that we don't know the answer to every question, that astrology is not a prophylactic against suffering, and that our power to help is limited.

Healing our shadow enables us to mend those planetary archetypes that have been torn into opposite halves and tragically pitted against one another. By opening to the possibility of failure (Saturn), uncertainty (Jupiter), and woundedness (Pluto), astrologers establish a more authentic relationship with these planets and give them a chance to heal. In so doing, the compensatory falseness of their counterfeit expression is removed, their extremism mitigated, and their buried potentials recovered. There is irony in healing the astrologer's shadow. For only by humbling ourselves before our clients do we become truly powerful; and only by admitting our ignorance do we become truly wise.

Chapter 2

Astro-Analyzing Dr. Laura

THE WOUNDED-HEALER ARCHETYPE

For many years, Dr. Laura Schlessinger has been the reigning champion of talk-radio, displacing both Howard Stern and Rush Limbaugh as the most listened-to-personality on the air. Broadcasting over 500 stations with 20 million people tuning in every day, Dr. Laura dispels quasi-religious advice and berates callers for their moral turpitude. A recently converted Orthodox Jew and poster-girl for the Christian right, Dr. Laura is an advocate of religion—any religion. Her latest book, *The Ten Commandments,* reflects her belief that she is a prophet of God. As she told *Vanity Fair,* "By virtue of what I do and how I live, I give evidence of God's presence on earth."

Her strategy for revealing God's presence is to deliver moral lectures from her radio pulpit with all the force of an armor-piercing shell. Whether she's launching into a shrill tirade against abortion, flying into a paroxysm of rage over pre-marital sex, or castigating feminists because they allegedly "hate being woman," Dr. Laura is on a tear. Her mission? To reverse the anything-goes mores of the 60's. Declaring her values "an oasis in the middle or a moral nothingness," she told *Radio Guide USA*, "I'm single-handedly trying to change this lack of values and ethics." Her tactics, however, often leave callers feeling bruised and brutalized. "How stupid can you be and still chew your food?" she berates one man. Another is scolded for being "gutless." A 20-year-old girl is reprimanded for having friends that are "drunken sluts." "Get a backbone transplant here!" she yells at an unmarried woman who has just moved in with her lover.

Yet, Dr. Laura has her own problems. Having insulted the gay community with her claim that homosexuality is a "mistake of God" and "biological error," Dr. Laura nearly lost a deal with Paramount to have her own TV show. Throughout 2000, there was a groundswell of public opinion organized against her. Actress Susan Sarandon posted a message on StopDrLaura.com: "I'm totally against wasting the airwaves by giving visibility to a person who is clearly in dire need of compassion, education and a good shrink herself." And Senator Bill Bradley said in a radio interview that Schlessinger's views "make me sick to my stomach." Mark Leno, supervisor for the city of San Francisco, wrote: "When Dr. Laura equates homosexuality with pedophilia, incest and bestiality she not only reveals her ignorance, heartlessness and inhumanity, she shames all of us who are fellow Jews and people of faith. That is why over 100 rabbis, priests, ministers and religious directors have denounced her evil tongue and her abusive use of the Bible and Torah. Only an equally cruel and foolish Paramount would offer her greater exposure."*

This is harsh stuff and one can only admire Dr. Laura's willingness to be pilloried while taking an uncompromising stand for what she believes. It is certainly a rare trait in today's culture of political

---

* See www.StopDrLaura.com for these and other comments in response to Dr. Laura's attacks on the gay community.

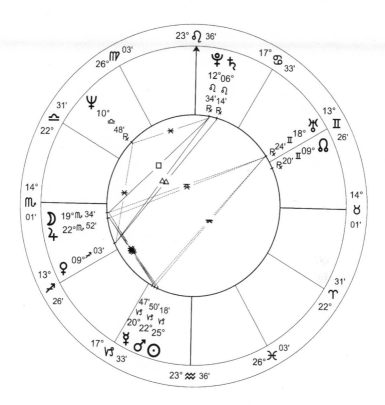

Figure 3: Dr Laura Schlessinger, Jan 16, 1947, New York, NY
(2:00am, speculative birth time)

correctness. Whether you love her or hate her, there is no question that Dr. Laura is a powerful voice. To many she is an American heroine who has taken a courageous stand against the do-what-you-feel mentality that has plunged our country into a moral quagmire. To others she is the Queen of Hate Radio, a Talk Show Dominatrix delivering sadistic blows to legions of masochistic callers. Perhaps a more objective way of assessing Dr. Laura is to examine her astrological chart, for it reveals without judgment the archetypal forces that animate her compelling personality.*

MARS UP THE YIN-YANG

Dr. Laura's Mars is conjunct her Sun (see Figure 3, previous page). This symbolizes an identity wedded to the archetype of the warrior. Her self-esteem (Sun) derives from an ability to fight for her own self-interest, and Mars is the perfect ally in combat. The emphasis is on strength, assertion, and autonomy. In effect, Dr. Laura's ego is a turbo-charged, lean-mean-fighting-machine that would rather confront her callers than win them over with sensitivity or caring. In *Vanity Fair* she is described as "tense, coiled, and ready to pounce." Dr. Laura herself says, "I'm like a panther." A fitness buff, she lifts weights every morning at 5:30, has a black belt in karate, and drives a Harley Davidson motorcycle. At the end of each show she frequently exhorts her listeners with a catchphrase that reflects her Martian sensibilities: "Now, go take on the day!"

As aspect derives its meaning from the sign (angle) to which it corresponds in the natural zodiac. Conjunctions have an Aries quality, for there is, in effect, no angle between them. The meaning of Aries and the conjunction are nearly identical. Accordingly, it cannot be overemphasized how powerful this conjunction is to Mars, for a Mars conjunction has a double Aries connotation: (1) it is a conjunction, and (2) it involves the ruler of Aries—Mars. When you consider that it as a double conjunction, involving Mercury and the Sun, it is powerful indeed. Mars gives Dr. Laura's will and intellect a direct, fearless, combative, irrepressible vitality.

With Mercury, Mars, and Sun all in Capricorn, it's not surprising

---

* As I have been unable to obtain a birth time for Dr. Laura, the following analysis is based solely on planetary signs positions and aspects. I have, however, created a speculative birth time of 2am that seems consistent with her life and character.

that Dr. Laura's values are ultra-conservative. Capricorn not only describes *how* Dr. Laura thinks (Mercury), asserts (Mars), and expresses herself (Sun); it also describes *what* she thinks about, fights for, and identifies with. Over and again she drills into her listener's brains that they won't find happiness in doing their own thing, but in (Capricorn) virtues of duty, responsibility, and self-discipline. To critics who argue that Schlessinger browbeats callers with puritanical advice, she responds: "We have 4,000 years of history of these values. They're not exactly mine. I'm conveying them. Is there something wrong in what I said, that you're supposed to honor your obligations above your immediate needs?"[1]

SMASH MOUTH THERAPY

Listening to Dr. Laura, one might be put off by her biting approach and often-brutal condemnation of listener's behavior. However, it is difficult not to respect her consistency, clarity, and forth-rightness. She cuts to the heart of caller's problems and often follows up with monologues that elaborate on a moral or psychological principle. Yet, I suspect that her obsession with Martian excesses—e.g., self-ishness, impulsivity, and egocentricity—belies her own tendencies in this regard. In other words, the very behaviors that Dr. Laura rails against may be a projection of her own faults, i.e., her *shadow*.

Evidence of this can be found on a number of levels. First, Dr. Laura doesn't just talk to callers, she snarls, scolds, and ridicules— what I call "smash mouth therapy" (she may be its only exponent). Her slashing, vituperative style is, indeed, like a panther going for the jugular. This implies only one way to live—*her way*. Critics may question whether this obey-me approach is truly constructive. It is, however, certainly consistent with her strong Mars emphasis. Mars takes action; it symbolizes the verb *to do*. So when it conjuncts the Sun the individual can be prone to impatient, pushy behavior. "Do this now!" Mars seems to be saying. Applied to therapy, it gives a penchant for a quick-fix mentality, as if all problems lend themselves to simple answers and immediate solutions. Dr. Laura is quick to remind her callers, however, that what she is doing is *not* therapy. "This is not a mental-health show," she once told *U.S. News & World Report.* "It's a moral health show."

The Capricorn flavor of her triple conjunction not only inclines Dr. Laura to morally conservative positions, it also underscores her natural presumption of authority. She hates it when callers challenge her command. "Shut up," she told one caller. "You asked for my opinion. Why would you argue with me?" A good psychotherapist, however, supports people in finding their own answers. Admittedly, this is not realistic in a talk show format in which Dr. Laura fields dozens of calls in a single hour. The point is that Sun/Mercury conjunct Mars is better suited to telling people *what to do* rather than support clients in a lengthy process of self-discovery. Accordingly, her Capricorn method is dictatorial and formulaic: *Obey God's laws!*

Dr. Laura also tends to be impulsive in the way that she responds to calls. Rather than considering the context and subtleties of a person's predicament, she will jump in with an immediate diagnosis. Many psychologists denounce her for making rapid-fire assessments and tongue-lashings after listening to callers for only a couple of minutes or even seconds. In effect, Dr. Laura is prone to premature interpretation. Like its sexual counterpart, she explodes and finishes before callers have had a chance to explain the facts, leaving them frustrated and longing for meaning.

Her strongly Martian nature seems to be saying, "There is only me, here, now. I'm the expert, and action must be taken immediately and decisively!" Not surprisingly, Dr. Laura terminated her private therapy practice in 1993 because she could no longer tolerate being a "blank slate" for clients. Now, she is extremely critical, even "ashamed" of her profession. She believes that psychology has done society a disservice by creating a national feelings fetish that breeds immature behavior. Note that Capricorn, as the sign opposed to Cancer, is the antithesis of tender, nonjudgmental acceptance of feelings. To Dr. Laura, feelings are less important than character. "In the last 20 years," she says, "we've erected a monument to feelings and made them the vantage point from which to make decisions. That's dangerous."[2] On the other hand, her rigid, rule-bound application of traditional values is a testament to Capricorn.

DESTROYS HER COMPETITION

Mars, of course, is the planet of aggression, whereas Capricorn signifies drive, determination, and ambition. Mars conjunct Mercury and the Sun in Capricorn is aggressively ambitious *in the extreme*. Picture a pumped-up black-belt in karate wired on amphetamines with teeth bared and sword drawn racing toward you on a Harley. That's a pretty good picture of how Dr. Laura attacks her goals. "My mission in life was to be very successful and brilliant at something," Schlessinger admits.

Yet, in Dr. Laura's ascent up the proverbial ladder of success, she's clawed and climbed over more than a few bodies. According to *Vanity Fair's* Leslie Bennett, "Scratch the surface of the radio industry, and the ill will toward her bursts like a festering boil."[3] Shelly Herman, a writer who worked with Schlessinger and been a close friend for many years, claims that any on-air personality that could conceivably be perceived as a rival was targeted for annihilation. "Tracey Miller, Marilyn Kagan, Barbara De Angelis, Mother Love—she systematically set out to destroy each of these women," says Herman. "She was the most vengeful, evil person."[4]

Herman's allegations that Dr. Laura is a "vengeful, evil person" may also reflect the strong Scorpio emphasis in Schlessinger's chart. With Moon conjunct Jupiter in Scorpio it's not surprising that Dr. Laura's career is characterized by Scorpio themes. Scorpio symbolizes the need for healing and transformation, and thus Scorpionic careers frequently involve work in the helping professions. Naturally drawn toward the dark side—i.e., toward that which is wounded or corrupt, Scorpio is associated with things hidden, forbidden, or taboo. Accordingly, for fear of reprisal, it does not operate openly. Scorpio's *modus operandi* is akin to tactical maneuvers. While it can be calculating, it is almost never direct or spontaneous. Strategic, as in acts of war, is more the Scorpio style. With both her Moon and Jupiter in Scorpio, Dr. Laura's strategy for gaining influence may involve surreptitious maneuvers to consolidate her power.

Marilyn Kagan, a psychotherapist who worked at the same station as Dr. Laura, alleges that Schlessinger tried to get her fired by planting stories that Kagan was physically ill and would probably end up in a hospital unable to work. When that tactic failed, Dr. Laura tried to undermine Kagan's authority by attacking her positions on the air. Kagan adds, "The sickest thing about Laura is how she ingratiates herself to you, with a plan: If I kiss your ass, then I can stab you in the back. The minute she didn't need people anymore, she would shit on them. She is such an evil, vicious human being. This woman is very ill; her envy is so perverse."[5]

DR. LAURA'S FAMILY OF ORIGIN

Psychologists generally believe that what we call "evil" is the outward manifestation of an unhealed wound; the pain, fear, and distrust that results from the wound can give rise to hostile, vindictive behavior. Again, this is typical of Scorpio. According to Dr. Laura, she grew up in a home (Moon) with little love. There was constant bickering and screaming between the parents, and her father was described as "physically and verbally abusive." Dr. Laura's mother was said to be "filled with negativity," perhaps as a result of spousal abuse.[6] Although Dr. Laura admonishes her callers to mend family rifts, she hasn't seen her own mother in 14 years and has been estranged from her sister, who is a psychotherapist, for more than twenty.

Note that Dr. Laura's Moon in Scorpio is quincunx Uranus. Because Uranus has to do with change, it can create instabilities in whatever planet it aspects. Certainly this could correlate to an unstable family life with frequent disruptions and emotional upsets. Uranus quincunx the Moon could symbolize a family and/or mother (Moon) that is emotionally labile, perhaps due to shocking events that overwhelmed the family/mother's capacity to cope. Since the Moon rules Cancer, and Uranus rules Aquarius, and Cancer and Aquarius are quincunx in the natural zodiac, this relationship dynamic is especially emphasized in Dr. Laura's chart since her Moon is *actually* quincunx Uranus. Thus a fundamental, archetypal challenge in the natural zodiac is highlighted. A quincunx often presents a dilemma. In this case, how can one have a close, loving family (Moon) *and* be open to unexpected changes that may disrupt family life (Uranus)? Emotional cut-offs are typical, as in the case of Dr. Laura's estrangement from her mother and sister.

A forerunner of this occurred with Dr. Laura's mother. The Moon, of course, symbolizes the mother, and aspects to the Moon often correlate to significant events in the mother's own life. A hard aspect from Uranus to the Moon suggests that the mother might have suffered an emotional rupture with her own family, which was actually the case. As an Italian war bride who married an American soldier, Dr. Laura's mother, Yolanda Ceccovini, had to leave her native Italy and move to New York. When her in-laws, who were Jewish, discovered that their son, Monroe, had married a Catholic girl, they cruelly rejected the young couple. From 1945 on, the Schlessingers were cut-off from both extended families—Yolanda's in Italy, and Monroe's in Brooklyn.

In effect, the marriage was cursed from the start. When loving your wife causes strife with your family of origin, it's a set-up for a son to feel guilty—guilty that he has hurt his parents, and guilty that his parents have hurt his wife. Likewise, when loving your husband causes banishment from his own family, Yolanda was vulnerable to guilt, too. In both instances, the guilt that resulted must have acted like a toxic, corrosive agent that ate away at whatever affection existed between them. My guess is that Dr. Laura's dysfunctional family provided fertile soil for the emotional insensitivity that her critics say is unfailingly characteristic of her style. It is possible that painful emotional issues from the past are playing themselves out through her profession, which focuses on family conflicts. In effect, her style of response (Moon) may be affected by a tendency for emotional distancing.

To some degree, this is inevitable with a hard aspect from the Moon to Uranus. If integrated, it reflects an ability to perceive emotional issues with a healthy detachment, situating them in a broader context and responding in a way that promotes necessary change. As stated, an aspect derives its meaning from the nature of the sign (angle) to which it corresponds. In Dr. Laura's chart, her Moon forms an *opening* quincunx to Uranus; thus, this aspect corresponds to the sign of Virgo.* One could say that Dr. Laura's specialty is family/emotional (Moon) *problems* (Virgo) that are caused by a lack of perspective (Uranus). For example, she is sensitive to the effects that dual income families have on the raising of children, and often exhorts mothers to adjust their lifestyles so they can stay at home until children enter school.

However, to the extent that Schlessinger's Moon-Uranus

---

* To determine whether an aspect is opening or closing, first note which planet is the faster moving planet, e.g., the Moon is faster than Uranus. Then note whether the faster moving planet is approaching the opposition point or the conjunction point of the two planets. For example, Moon in Scorpio is 150 degrees ahead of Uranus in Gemini, thus this would be an *opening* (or lower) quincunx. If the Moon is in Capricorn, it is again 150 degrees away from Uranus in Gemini, but now it would be a *closing* (or upper) quincunx and have a Scorpio flavor, i.e., an aspect of crisis, wounding, and repression.

quincunx is *not* integrated, then her emotions will tend to be unstable, vacillating between *over*emotional responses characterized by a loss of perspective, or dry intellectual ones characterized by a loss of feeling. Problems and dilemmas that accrue from the conflict between Moon and Uranus will tend to be an area of obsessional (Virgonian) focus, e.g., complications stemming from ruptured family ties, faulty child-rearing, family upheavals, hurt feelings, and the like.

Also, if Schlessinger is "acting out" a wound from her family (Moon) by projecting her Moon Scorpio, then there is likely to be the perception of evil in the outside world. In this case, Dr. Laura will be inclined to perceive a lack of support of caring. She may then think that *she* is the one who has been wronged, in which case Scorpio can be cruel and vindictive. When Laurie Sanders, who worked at the same station as Dr. Laura, complained that Dr. Laura's child, Deryk, was screaming and laughing at the top of his lungs during Sander's radio broadcast, Dr. Laura was livid. Later when Sanders was mysteriously let go (allegedly because of budget cuts), Schlessinger reportedly ran around overjoyed, singing, 'Ding, dong, the witch is dead!'

Such actions need to be understood, however, in the context of the wound that underlies the behavior. Scorpionic hostility is actually an attempt to rid oneself of pain and shame by evoking in the other what is subjectively felt within. It is a projection of "badness" outward into the other person. Instead of embracing one's pain and seeking to heal it, the source of the pain is externalized and then subjugated. In other words, an external threat is substituted for an internal fear, and an external solution is sought over an internal one.

Accordingly, if Dr. Laura is sufficiently convinced that the *other* person is evil, she might rationalize "the end justifies the means" and get in the first blow. Such an act may appear completely unprovoked. In fact, when Schlessinger found out something she could use against a rival, she exploited it in full measure. Colleagues were appalled by these tactics. "If you're the best, earn the job—don't go digging up dirt," said one. "To go out and discredit someone to get what you want—is that ethical?" asks Laurie Sanders. "She was always looking at it like 'This should be mine—and I will do whatever it takes to make that mine.'"[7] My guess is that Dr. Laura rationalized these tactics by convincing herself that it was her rivals who were trying to gain an unfair advantage in hopes of deposing her. Anyone with a strong Mars component to their personality accepts as a matter of course that life is a competition and only the strong survive.

To the extent that she is projecting her fears, however, her behavior helps to bring about the conditions she anticipates. "Everyone who's known her hates her," says Marilyn Kagan, the radio host who incurred Schlessinger's enmity.[8] "She is probably the unhappiest woman I've ever met," adds Shelly Herman. Dr. Norton Kristy, another prominent psychologist who shared radio duties with Schlessinger, says: "She is not a nice person to the people around her...Laura is mean-spirited, and in my personal direct knowledge, is mean-spirited with her father, her mother, her sister, her husband."[9]

Taken collectively, this is powerful testimony. Yet, there is no way of knowing to what extent these criticisms might be, at least in part, motivated by envy. Also, it is important to understand the factors that underlay Dr. Laura's behavior. If she experienced her family of origin as unstable, unpredictable, or erratic in some way, or if either she or her parents experienced a significant rupture of family ties, then Schlessinger may be fixated on the possibility that similar traumatic upsets may occur in the future. A common way of defending against this is to turn a passive experience into an active one, i.e., do to the other what has been done to you. In other words, Dr. Laura can launch a pre-emptive strike by severing a relationship before the other person does it to her. In this way, she gains an illusion of control over the thing feared.

There is some evidence that this has occurred. I mentioned that she has not seen her mother or sister for nearly two decades.* In addition to cutting herself off from immediate family, Dr. Laura has left behind a string of broken friendships and professional relationships. Her first mentor in the radio industry, talk-show host Bill Ballance, not only gave Schlessinger her start in 1975, but was also her boyfriend for several years. Yet in 1995 when the retired Ballance was invited to work on Schlessinger's current station, KFI, Dr. Laura threatened to quit if they hired him. "Talk about payback for Bill's kindness and generosity," says former colleague, Dr. Norton Kristy. "Having opened doors for her and fundamentally created her career for her, it was a savagely mean-spirited return. But that's Laura."[10] Of course, there may be more to the story than we can know. Another former friend, Shelly Herman, says that Dr. Laura "doesn't seem to have a guilty conscience, even though we know the road is littered with people. Maybe that's why she's not happy: she knows from whence she came."

Again, however, we can understand this in the context of her Moon-Uranus quincunx, which is like growing up on a fault line; the family home would be subject to periodic tremors, earthquakes, and aftershocks.** If she was wounded by emotional ruptures in her own family of origin, this would sensitize her to emotional ruptures in the lives of those she is committed to help. Very often a child will assume that whatever happens in the family

---

* Also, until her mid-thirties, Dr. Laura did not want a family and was committed to not ever having children. According to *Vanity* Fair, this changed when she realized how unhappy she was. After deciding to have a baby, she underwent protracted fertility treatments to conceive.

** After writing this I learned that Dr. Laura's current home, in the San Fernando Valley, was burned almost to the ground in 1992. As if this wasn't enough, it was then severely damaged in the 1994 earthquake.

is somehow a consequence of her own behavior; hence, within any childhood trauma are seeds of unconscious guilt. Dr. Laura may project her guilt onto her callers, who are then castigated for any acts that are disruptive to *their* families. If Dr. does not practice what she preaches, this suggests that she is working out her neurotic conflicts through her callers.

Accordingly, she is emphatic in her opposition to pre-marital sex, abortions, divorces, working mothers, affairs, same sex marriages, or any other alternative lifestyle that, in her opinion, threatens the stability of the family unit. Consider this Dr. Laura invective: "Same-sex marriage is destructive to western civilization because it destroys the building block that is mom, dad, committed, heterosexual, monogamous, children." I suspect that the sense of mission Dr. Laura feels about preserving the stability of the nuclear family is compensatory for the traumatic instability she experienced in her own family.

That she is extraordinarily vulnerable to the threat of sudden loss was made painfully clear when her husband, Lew Bishop, nearly died after cardiac arrest. Schlessinger admits, "I was down on my knees...screaming in terror and anguish." She told *Vanity Fair* how she then began to suffer incapacitating panic attacks—"terror and pounding and thinking I'm going to die." Finally, at work, she completely collapsed moments before airtime. "She actually had a nervous breakdown right in front of all of us," marvels a former colleague. "She got in an argument with her screener, and all of a sudden she was down on the ground vibrating like a carp out of water."[11] Paramedics carried her out on a stretcher. Former colleague, Dr. Norton Kristy, writes: "My own observations were that Laura had experienced a great deal of childhood insecurity and need, and that it had left her with a rather hard outer shell in which she was sardonic and humorous, and pretended to a degree of tough-minded strength that really did not go very deep."[12]

YOD TO URANUS

A key factor in Schlessinger's chart is the yod that Uranus forms to her Scorpio and Capricorn planets. Whereas Mars and Mercury in Capricorn form a sextile to Jupiter and the Moon in Scorpio, each of these planets, in turn, quincunxes Uranus in Gemini. As the focal point of the yod, Uranus is under tremendous pressure to accommodate to the needs of the planets that quincunx it. For the aspect to work constructively, Uranus must find a way to adjust and transform itself to support a healthy expression of Mercury, Mars, Jupiter, and the Moon. Each of these planets, in turn, must accommodate itself to Uranus. Accordingly, Uranus is a central player in her chart (see Figure 4, page 60).

Under the best of circumstances, Uranus brings about change and reform by providing a broad, wholistic awareness that awakens the system to new possibilities. Uranus is the revolutionary; it shocks, reveals, startles, and finally frees the system—people, families, cultures—to evolve toward a more humane and enlightened perspective. As a liberator, Uranus is naturally associated with liberal perspectives, i.e., those that are permissive and progressive and which affirm that change is necessary for a system's further evolution. Liberalism is a theory founded on the potential perfectibility of human beings, even if that perfectibility requires excessive government intervention to realize it.

Ideally, each planet that Uranus aspects is made more progressive, radical, and open to change. Dr. Laura must find a way to be open-minded (Uranus-Mercury), able to fight for a cause (Uranus-Mars), broadminded in her acceptance of alternative values and opinions (Uranus-Jupiter), and capable of detaching from her emotions so that she is able to care for others in a way that liberates them from old, conditioned patterns (Uranus-Moon).

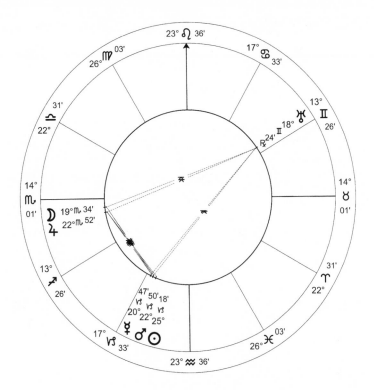

Figure 4: Dr Laura Schlessinger' yod

To the extent that she integrates the yod, Uranus will be utilized in a manner that solves problems and resolves crises that have to do with a *lack* of these very qualities, e.g., with Moon/Jupiter quincunx Uranus, she could solve family problems related to religious intolerance. Or, perhaps, she could correct child-care problems that she perceives as resulting from obsolete child-rearing practices. Conversely, to the extent that she does not integrate the yod to Uranus, she will tend to resist change, close her mind to what she perceives as radical perspectives, and express righteous indignation whenever she feels threatened by progressive developments within society. Assessment of how well Dr. Laura's has integrated her yod may have more to do with one's own political values than Dr. Laura herself.

A URANIAN REACTIONARY

Certainly, Dr. Laura is on a crusade to change America's values, especially those that pertain to the family and the raising of children (Uranus quincunx Moon-Jupiter).* "I am getting people to stop doing wrong and start doing right," she says. In front of her new, California Mission-style house in the San Fernando Valley is a sign that alludes to her lofty goals: ON A MISSION, it says. Some perceive her particular mission, however, as reactionary in its resistance to liberal and progressive elements within society (Uranus) that call for fundamental changes in our attitudes and laws (Jupiter). For example, Dr. Laura doesn't believe in religiously mixed marriages, which she calls "interfaithless marriages." Her husband, who used to be Episcopalian, was asked by Dr. Laura to convert to Orthodox Judaism, which is her adopted faith.

If Uranus is not well integrated, an individual may tend to resist the Uranian impulse. Resistance to Uranus produces the "reactionary"— someone characterized by reaction *against* change, progress, or liberalism. A reactionary is radically conservative and wants to return to traditional, well established values that have evolved over centuries if not millennia.

Unlike liberalism, which is opposed to conservative authority, a reactionary advocates for conservative laws through religious, legal, or political means. For example, Dr. Laura is vehemently opposed to gay rights and same-sex marriages and wants laws enacted that

---

* Contrary to many astrological texts, I associate "values" with Jupiter, since Jupiter is concerned with ethics, justice, and virtue. When we speak of moral values and the belief systems—religious and philosophical—that support them, we are talking Jupiter. A combination of Jupiter and the Moon would incline the individual to emphasize family (Moon) values.

forbid such unions. She rails against the raising of adopted children by gay parents, and denounces the American Psychological Association for removing homosexuality from its list of "mental disorders." To her, gay sex is "deviant" and individuals addicted to such should seek counseling. Her perorations strongly suggest that many gays are predators, eager to convert new members to the faith. Accordingly, she urges parents to avoid bringing kids into the company of possibly gay relatives.

From her on-air bully pulpit, Dr. Laura has taken on a number of sensitive social issues. In almost every case, she unabashedly champions the Christian Right's social agenda by dispensing a steady stream of anti-gay, anti-feminism ("they nauseate and sicken me"), anti-abortion propaganda. She bashes liberals of every variety and even advocates *against* hate-crimes legislation. In a recent broadcast, she savaged—by name—a Connecticut 8th grader who wrote an award winning essay in favor of free speech on the Internet. According to *Newsweek* magazine, Dr. Laura snarled "If she was my daughter, I'd probably put her up for adoption."[13] She then suggested that the girl be "sacrificed," Inca style.

For these and other comments, Dr. Laura was thunderously condemned by the Canadian Broadcast Standards Council for what it called "abusively discriminatory" violations of Canada's broadcast code. The council also rebuked Canadian radio stations that broadcast Dr. Laura's show and will require them to censor anti-gay comments she makes on future broadcasts. Radio stations that carry her show will be required to broadcast statements on the ruling at prime time – in effect, warning Canadian listeners against Schlessinger's ideas, which were likened to racism.[14]

REPETITION COMPULSION

I leave it to the reader to decide the extent to which Dr. Laura has integrated her yod to Uranus. On the one hand, it appears that Dr.

Laura is a reactionary; on the other, that she is a courageous voice in the wilderness drawing attention to the dark side of liberal, progressive values. It is interesting to recall one manifestation of Dr. Laura's yod during her childhood. Remember that Schlessinger's father, who was Jewish, married an Italian war bride, who was Catholic. The father's family reacted poisonously, cutting him off from 1945 to the end of his life in 1990, when he died of stomach (Moon) cancer. Forty-five years of bitter hatred because the woman he married was not Jewish! We can only surmise the effect this had on the marriage, and how this, in turn, affected the children. Schlessinger's parents eventually divorced.

It would appear that Dr. Laura's Jupiter-Moon quincunx to Uranus symbolized the lack of religious tolerance that was so damaging to her own family. The Moon, of course, symbolizes family, whereas Jupiter is religion. Uranus signifies, among other things, an attitude of tolerance and is fundamentally concerned with the inevitability of change. If integrated, this could manifest as a willingness for couples of different faiths to marry and adopt a new, non-denominational approach to religion. However, with both Moon and Jupiter quincunx Uranus, Dr. Laura's extended family suffered a deep schism between their religious allegiance on the one hand, and a need for tolerance and change on the other.

A quincunx is an aspect of incompatibility between two functions that seem to have nothing in common. If not integrated, an opening quincunx can result in a perpetual problem that results from the disintegration of the two functions. When Dr. Laura's grandparents disowned her father and rejected his wife, they were saying, "We cannot tolerate you or accept change; we have nothing in common." The Moon's placement in Scorpio only underscores the intensity of the wound that resulted from this ostracism.

A central tenet of psychology is that people have a compulsion to repeat traumatic events from childhood. Repetition compulsion is the impulse to repeat distressing, even painful, situations during the course of one's life without recognizing one's own participation in bringing about such incidents. Freud recognized that repetition in action is a way of remembering, i.e., it substitutes for verbal recollection of forgotten memories.

Repetition compulsion has two forms, passive and active. In the passive form, the individual makes decisions that lead to a re-experiencing of the original traumatic event, e.g., if a girl was physically abused by a parent, she might marry a man who is physically abusive. In the active form, the individual turns a passive experience into an active one, thereby repeating the experience but by reversing roles. A forerunner of this occurs in children's play when they act out passively experienced traumatic events in an attempt to gain mastery over them. An adult will do this simply by treating others the way she was treated. Such behavior is compensatory in that the individual gains as much distance as possible from the feared experience. By identifying with the perpetrator, the individual dis-identifies with being the victim, as if to say, "You can't hurt me anymore; I hurt *you!*"

An active version of repetition compulsion would be Dr. Laura's condemnation of mixed ("interfaithless") marriages. In one show, a Christian woman reported to Dr. Laura that she was engaged to an Islamic man. As this woman thought family members should be of the same faith, she was considering becoming a Muslim, yet, still believed in Jesus. Dr. Laura told her to end the relationship because "false vows are an affront to God" and "the marriage will never work." In other words, Dr. Laura advocated that the caller do to her fiancée what Dr. Laura's grandparents did to her family. The caller was devastated.

For many years, Schlessinger didn't believe in any religion. However, in the last decade she evolved from a non-believer into a Conservative Jew and now, finally, an Orthodox Jew. Orthodox Judaism is the most formal, rigid, and literal of Jewish movements. Orthodox Jews believe that God gave Moses *all* the laws—the whole Torah—which are absolutely true, complete, and unchangeable. That Dr. Laura is drawn to a doctrine that presumes a strict and absolute certainty may be compensatory for an underlying *uncertainty* that is characteristic of Jupiter quincunx Uranus. Uranus tends naturally to rebel against orthodox doctrines. However, if the individual repudiates Uranus itself, then just the opposite occurs: *ultra-traditional beliefs* as a defense against Uranian values. As the focal point of a yod, Uranus constitutes both a problem and a crisis for Dr. Laura. Her manner of resolving it is the challenge of her life.

In adopting her paternal grandparent's faith, Dr. Laura has, in effect, identified with the aggressor. This is not a criticism of Judaism; it is a commentary on the psychological motivations that influenced her choice of faiths. Dr. Laura's strong opposition liberal causes, feminism, and other social issues may simply be a repetition of the bigotry and divisiveness that characterized her childhood.

On the other hand, some might view Dr. Laura's opposition to gay rights and same-sex marriages as a long overdue corrective to an attitude of tolerance that has morphed into moral endorsement. "In Genesis," she says, "God didn't get Adam another guy." In another show she protests, "The debate over gay rights – Rights. RIGHTS! RIGHTS? For sexually deviant behavior there are now rights? Why does deviant sexual behavior get rights? Man-on-man and woman-on-woman sexual activity is a deviant sexual orientation, and does not promote any of the values set forth biblically."[15]

In order to combat Schlessinger's disapproval, the Gay and Lesbian Alliance Against Defamation (GLAAD) met with producers of her upcoming TV show. GLAAD Communications Director Stephen Spurgeon laid out the organization's problems with Dr. Laura: "It's really three points: One is her vocabulary and the terminology that she uses; secondly, she only cites conservative sources, like the Family Research Council; and third, she just has a lack of respect for any view unlike her own."

It is this last remark that drives the point home. The problem is not merely Schlessinger's views, it is her seeming intolerance for any view other than her own. Just as her paternal grandparents rejected their daughter-in-law merely because she was different, so Dr. Laura is rejecting ideas that she perceives as different. Granted, her rejection is not simply discriminatory, but based on religious and moral values that she regards as conducive to the greater good. If she was able to have a reasoned discussion about such matters rather than use her show as a bully pulpit to shrilly denounce liberal causes, she would not be such a lightning rod for controversy and might even be more successful in convincing others of the merit of her opinion.

MARS-JUPITER INFLAMMATORY RHETORIC

I have already mentioned how Dr. Laura's triple conjunction—Mars, Mercury, and Sun in Capricorn—inclines her to identify with conservative values. However, that is not the whole story. The fact that Mars sextiles her Jupiter-Moon conjunction is especially significant in light of the militancy of her views. Note that Mars and Jupiter are only 6 minutes shy of an exact sextile! Mars is the warrior archetype and is naturally combative. Jupiter is the guru—a teacher and guide in spiritual matters. Whereas Mars wants to do its own thing, Jupiter is concerned with what is right for the community. When these two planets combine, the individual may assume: "what's right for me is right for everyone!"

The aspect suggests an ardent interest in philosophical matters, especially as these pertain to familial duties and obligations

(Moon). Mars inflames and strengthens one's convictions. Once a truth is embraced, the person is likely to assert it with a vengeance. Accordingly, this is the aspect of the Holy Crusader—someone who fights for the truth. Mars renders Dr. Laura's religious convictions more spirited and aggressive. However, as *Vanity Fair* writer Leslie Bennetts suggests, Dr. Laura's followers aren't really seeking religion: they want a taskmaster to stiffen their spines and tell them what to do. "And Dr. Laura is happy to oblige, dispensing her advice in doses that land as hard as a cane on the back….She is like an avenging fury, come to reveal the path to righteousness."[16] Schlessinger's fervor is indisputably evangelical. And in an age of moral relativity, her certitude compels. Listeners regard her as a paragon of virtue, a beacon of hope in a dissolute, degraded world. In short, a Mars-Jupiter sextile gives Dr. Laura the courage of her convictions.

The extreme emotional fervor with which a belief is held is often evidence of a reaction formation, i.e., a painful idea or feeling, which is unconscious, is replaced in conscious awareness by its opposite. If, for example, Dr. Laura secretly doubts that there is any overarching purpose or intelligence in the Universe, she may react to this by proclaiming absolute faith in the indubitable truth of Biblical Scripture. A reaction formation is marked by extravagant showiness—she protests *too* much—and by compulsiveness. Extreme forms of behavior of any kind usually denote a reaction formation. We already know that only a short time ago Dr. Laura didn't believe in *any* religion. *Now* she is an Orthodox Jew—about as far right as one can go. This suggests that her conversion is actually a reaction formation—a defense against her own religious doubt.

MARS-URANUS: SPEARHEADING CHANGE

As the warrior archetype, Mars arouses, inflames, and emboldens any planet it aspects. A mars-aspected planet is rendered more aggressive and *encouraged* to assert itself, for better or worse. With Mars conjunct Mercury, Dr. Laura is known for her sharp tongue and cutting remarks. Her mind is quick and her speech forceful, typical of Mars.

The red planet also makes a closing quincunx to Uranus as part of Dr. Laura's yod. Since Uranus symbolizes change, progress, and revolution, Mars makes this impulse more combative. Mars-Uranus is the social activist—someone who is willing *to take action* and fight to bring about social changes. An activist, however, is not content merely to take individual action (Mars), but may galvanize the collective and spearhead mass movements (Uranus) as a means of opposing or supporting a controversial issue. Perhaps more than any other aspect, Mars-Uranus has an incendiary quality. It's the rabble rouser who stirs things up, inflames people's passions, and incites them to rebel. Schlessinger's use of talk radio to assert her social agenda is itself an expression of Mercury-Mars quincunx Uranus in Gemini (the talk sign). In US Online News, Amy Bernstein writes "This radio talk-show host is as outraged as Rush Limbaugh and as outspoken as G. Gordon Liddy—two leading voices of the conservative revolution. Dr. Laura is the personal, nonpolitical side of that revolution."[17]

As stated, Dr. Laura's relationship to Uranus is extremely problematic. The only aspects it makes are the four quincunxes to Moon, Jupiter, Mercury, and Mars. As the quincunx is an aspect of repression, Uranus is thrown into shadow. Accordingly, Dr. Laura is tuned into the dark side of Uranus as encapsulated in the well-known maxim: *the road to hell is paved with good intentions*. For example, she boldly exposes what she regards as the dangers of excessive tolerance and moral endorsement of homosexuality: "A huge portion of the male homosexual populace is predatory on young boys," she charges, and goes on to warn of a militant gay conspiracy: "you people have to get off your duffs, or you're going to lose your country to fascism."[18]

However, this may merely be a projection of Schlessinger's own militant, fascist tendencies. Fascism, which is the antithesis of liberalism, is marked by a centralization of authority under dictatorial, oppressive control. It is usually characterized by belligerent racism and suppression of opposition through terror and censorship. In a recent article, "Call to Arms," Dr. Laura admitted she liked it when the National Guard occupied her hometown of Los Angeles following the earthquake in 1994. "There they were, it seemed, on every corner—uniformed, armed, ammunition slung across their chests, ready. As I recall, there was absolutely no crime in Los Angeles at that time...I went on the air and said, 'Gee, why can't these guys just stay here?' and everyone freaked out."[19]

Recognizing that we can't count on the dubious blessings of armed occupation, Dr. Laura suggested an alternative: we should all get guns and arm ourselves to protect America from "child killers, killer children, private militias, home-grown and imported terrorists, to say nothing of old-fashioned, garden variety psychopaths and criminals – all armed and dangerous and now encouraged, educated in evil and joined in unholy conspiracy on the World Wide Web."[20] In various other publications she aggressively advocates against abortion, feminists, gay rights initiatives, hate crimes legislation, free speech on the Internet, and so on. All of this has created a backlash, as occurred on March 21st when over 500 protesters descended on Paramount Studios in Hollywood to demand that Paramount executives cancel the upcoming Dr. Laura TV show.

The closing quincunx from Mars to Uranus has a Scorpio quality, being an aspect of crisis, wounding, and danger. There is likely to be an unconscious conflict between individual self-interest (Mars) versus the collective good (Uranus), and between the need for survival versus forces of social change. These different drives are apt to be perceived as mutually exclusive. Progressive social movements (Uranus) could be seen as threatening to individual survival (Mars); thus, they must be vehemently attacked and resisted. While Dr. Laura sees danger lurking in every liberal-progressive corner, others feel it is Dr. Laura herself who is dangerous. David Lee, a writer and producer on *Frasier*, attacked his own studio when he spoke to hundreds of protesters at the company's Hollywood lot to demand that the Dr. Laura show be shelved. "It is outrageous that Paramount chooses to be in business with a woman who is dangerous to the gay community," Lee said. "She may not have a club in her hand but she encourages an atmosphere where those who do wield weapons feel free to use them."[21]

A RADAR SCREEN FOR EVIL

I have already mentioned how Jupiter conjunct the Moon gives Dr. Laura a penchant for family values. That Jupiter and the Moon are both in Scorpio makes this combination particularly intense. The Moon is our automatic listening response. Its sign position and aspects reveal how we receive information, connect on a feeling level, and respond in a caring way. Because Scorpio symbolizes the need for transformation, it is naturally attracted to what is hidden or repressed. Moon Scorpio, therefore, can associate feelings with danger, risk and taboo. There may be a fear that feelings are potentially destructive. Scorpio symbolizes the shadow, the daimonic; thus Moon Scorpio worries that feelings may erupt and possess the person and cause him/her to do something shameful. Because Scorpio is sexual energy, feelings can also be eroticized. Consequently, they are often repressed, and like some dragon hidden deep within a cave, lurk just below the surface of consciousness.

All of this is consistent with Dr. Laura's attitude toward feelings. For example, she argues that psychology has overblown the importance of feelings. Making decisions on the mood of the moment is a prime reason that American society is unraveling, says Dr. Laura. "I'm very big on feelings," she says, "I'm a well of feelings. But that's not how I make decisions because if I did, every time I felt angry I'd hit somebody and every I felt happy [aroused] I'd go to bed with somebody."[22] Note also in this statement the implicit conflict between her Capricornian values and Cancerian sentiments. With her Sun, Mars, and Mercury all conjunct in Capricorn, Dr. Laura is a veritable spokesperson for Capricornian self-restraint as an antidote to Cancerian emotional excesses.

Despite the probable repression of feelings, Moon Scorpio is an excellent listener, perhaps too excellent. Moon Scorpio hears things that were never meant to be communicated. There is an extraordinary depth and penetration into hidden areas. Perceptions are keen, sharp, piercing. Yet, there can be a suspiciousness that borders on paranoia. When a female caller denied that fear of being alone was the reason she couldn't leave her boyfriend, Schlessinger exploded: "You're lying! You're wrong! You don't want to face that it's your inadequacy!" While Dr. Laura may not always be on target, she seems to have a radar-like sensing mechanism that enables her to ferret out the real motivations behind a caller's concern. When a response does come, it can be of such cold and ruthless intensity that it at once exposes and transforms the listener.

Her agenda, however, is clearly not to therapize her callers. "This is not a shrink show," Schlessinger asserts. "I'm preaching, teaching, and nagging. That's what I do." In this regard, the Moon's conjunction with Jupiter in Scorpio reveals *how* and *what* Dr. Laura teaches. Jupiter, of course, is the teacher-preacher of the planetary pantheon. As ruler of Sagittarius, Jupiter's mission is to spread justice, truth, and virtue. Above all, Jupiter is concerned with values, by which I mean ethics—the codification of morality. Depending upon Jupiter's aspects, different values and truths are emphasized. Each planet constitutes a separate domain with its own virtues. For Mars, strength and courage are paramount. For Mercury, education is most valued. With Jupiter conjunct the Moon, Dr. Laura's is going to be especially concerned with values and virtues that fall within the Moon's domain. These include, of course, a focus on family and the raising of children. It is here that Dr. Laura's Scorpionic vitriolity is given full rein.

Regular listeners know well the list of no-no's that can provoke an on-air tongue-lashing: working mothers, infidelity, living together, premarital sex, "oopsie" pregnancies, and in-name-only parents. Yet, scads of offenders will call in, suffering their punishment with submissive deference. As the sign position of Jupiter, Scorpio describes *how* Dr. Laura proclaims her truths: powerfully, passionately, and with insight as sharp as a surgeon's scalpel. Whatever Jupiter in Scorpio believes, it believes with consuming intensity. It wants not merely to teach, but to transform, heal, and purge destructive ideas. The bottom line is that Jupiter in Scorpio wants to convert you. Accordingly, it is capable of courting disciples with evangelical fervor. One has only to visit Dr. Laura's web site to see evidence of this.

When combined with the Moon, Jupiter receives even greater emotional impetus. In an attempt to care and protect, lunar feelings are subordinated to Jupiterian beliefs, which launch powerful Scorpionic fusillades designed to eliminate sin and depravity. Jupiter-Moon in Scorpio wants to excoriate corrupt conditions that threaten the integrity of the family. If pure lunar feeling is subordinated to ethics, Jupiterian intellect is emotionalized. What Dr. Laura *thinks* is right, she *feels* strongly about; yet, rationality struggles to predominate. As Dr. Laura put it, "I don't really need to hear about your feelings. I assume you have them, and I assume you think they're the greatest thing in the Universe, but the reality is that regardless of your feelings, you're still commanded to be an ethical, compassionate, just person."[23]

Scorpio not only describes *how* Dr. Laura proclaims her truths, but *what* these truths are. At the highest level, Scorpio envisions a fully healed, regenerated system purged of its toxic elements. If Jupiter in Scorpio could speak, it might say, "I believe in a sacred power that is capable of transforming darkness into light." Accordingly, Dr. Laura is going to be preoccupied with the dark side—depravity, impropriety, perversion, betrayal, revenge—for that is the fodder of her mission. Whatever is regarded as bad, Jupiter in Scorpio will condemn and attack with the unerring accuracy of a cruise missile. Like a radar screen dialed in to pick up any evil that might be floating undetected in the social organism, Dr. Laura's Jupiter is primed and ready to expose. Not surprisingly, a prime target for her radar screen is sexuality.

Sooner or later, in every show, Dr. Laura will get around to preaching about sex. Topics sure to rile her are pre-marital sex (which she calls "shaking up"), and abortion (which she refers to as "sucking it into the sink"). She hates infidelity, especially philandering husbands who are referred to as scum, worms, and slime. Of course when the subject of homosexuality comes up, Dr. Laura can barely contain her hostility and disgust.

Other subjects certain to capture her attention include pedophilia, incest, sadomasochism, bestiality, and cross-dressing. The question is not whether these behaviors are wrong, but why they so unfailingly preoccupy Dr. Laura's attention. For she is not merely responding to listener's calls, but preaching, writing, and taking an aggressive activist stance in regard to such Scorpionic phenomena. At the end of each program, Dr. Laura exclaims, "Now, go do the right thing!"

SHADOW & HYPOCRISY

Innumerable sources hold that Dr. Laura is guilty in many instances of the very things she abhors in her callers. She's estranged from her sister and hasn't seen her mother in nearly 20 years, yet she berates callers for their failure to mend family strife. Dr. Laura preaches that gossip is a sin. Yet, she would routinely dig up or fabricate dirt about other radio hosts, then leak the incriminating information to their bosses with a particularly malicious spin. While she rails against divorce on her show, Schlessinger is herself divorced. Dr. Laura is a passionate opponent of premarital sex; yet, she lived with Lew Bishop for nine years before marrying him. Vehemently opposed to pregnancies out of wedlock, she was reportedly pregnant at her own wedding.[24] Schlessinger criticizes parents who insist on bearing biological offspring rather than adopting needy children, yet she herself underwent protracted fertility treatments to conceive her son.

Earlier I stated that Dr. Laura's Sun-Mars-Mercury conjunction might be at the root of her disdain for impulsive, irresponsible behavior—especially with regards to premarital sex and infidelity. That she might be projecting her own tendencies onto callers is supported by confessions of former mentor, Bill Ballance, who claims that Dr. Laura jumped into bed with him on their first date. Not only that, but she was married at the time, a fact she chose not to disclose to Ballance until months after their relationship began. Ballance alleges that Schlessinger was sexually forward. "We used to thrash around like a coupled of crazed weasels," he leered. "I used to call her Klu Klux, because she's a demon between the sheets." Proof of their affair was subsequently published on the Internet— the infamous "Dr. Laura's Dirty Dozen," twelve nude photos of Schlessinger that Ballance took when they were lovers. He declares that Dr. Laura not only requested that he shoot the photos, but insisted that they show full frontal nudity, including some very revealing close-ups. Ballance, who was a decorated marine captain and combat officer in WWII, quips that the most action he ever had was with Dr. Laura from 1975-1977.[25]

I suspect that Schlessinger's colleagues are intent on pointing out contradictions between what Dr. Laura says and what Dr. Laura does because of the apparent hypocrisy. Schlessinger admits there are "things I have regret and have shame for."[26] Yet, she refuses to discuss the particulars. "I see no reason to embarrass myself," she told Leslie Bennetts of *Vanity Fair*. While Dr. Laura might have changed, change is not necessarily the same thing as growth. The lack of compassion that typifies her responses to callers whose behavior mirrors her own is evidence of a reaction formation, i.e., a splitting of the wounded-healer archetype. We will explore this topic in our final section on Dr. Laura's Saturn-Pluto conjunction.

SATURN-PLUTO SHADOW: THE DOMINATRIX

As the dispositor of her Scorpio and Capricorn planets, Dr. Laura's Saturn-Pluto conjunction is particularly important, for the entire chart leads to it. A dispositor is a planet that rules the sign that another planet is *in*. Thus Schlessinger's Capricorn planets are disposited by Saturn, and her Scorpio planets are disposited by Pluto. Dispositors are like runners in a relay race; one planet hands off to the next—i.e., to its dispositor. The relationship is one of sequential unfoldment. In this case, Schlessinger's Capricorn planets trigger Saturn, and her Scorpio planets activate Pluto. Because each planet constitutes a type of action, the flow of dispositors symbolizes the structure of action. Every planet relies upon its dispositor to help it achieve its aims. Thus her Capricorn and Scorpio planets are relying on the Saturn-Pluto conjunction to carry forth their mission. But how capable is Saturn-Pluto of doing so?

When Pluto conjuncts a planet, that planet is subject to transformation. And whatever needs to be transformed (healed) is by definition wounded. Since Saturn signifies Dr. Laura's relationship to authority—the system, government, rules, order, structure, and career—this entire domain of activity is potentially thrown into shadow. Imagine that Pluto has abducted Saturn and dragged it down into the underworld. Such a condition would predispose one to believe that the system is corrupt, that order is crumbling, and that our political structure is descending into evil. With Saturn-Pluto there is often a deep distrust (Pluto) of authority (Saturn), and identification with those who have suffered an abuse of authority. Thus Saturn-Pluto may challenge the existing power structure; if the current regime is corrupt, then someone has to regenerate the system by purging it of its destructive elements. Otherwise the system (order, government, civilization) may disintegrate. Accordingly, Saturn-Pluto can symbolize an impulse to destroy, undermine, or reform the present system.

As stated, Pluto's job is to carry forward the agenda of the planets it disposits—in this case, the Moon and Jupiter. If Dr. Laura is concerned about principles (Jupiter) of child rearing (Moon), then her faith in Saturn—the government—to provide an adequate structure for the protection of families is likely to be sorely tested. If Saturn is wounded, as suggested by it's conjunction to Pluto, she may believe that the system is failing to control against practices that she perceives as immoral (Jupiter) and damaging to the family (Moon). Also, because Pluto-Saturn trines Dr. Laura's Venus, her concern will necessarily extend to the rules governing marriage and social relations in general. The trine suggests that Dr. Laura's power and authority can be effectively utilized in the service of intimacy and marriage.

I believe this is evident in her condemnation of the American Psychological Association for removing homosexuality from its list of "mental disorders," in her denunciation of state laws legalizing same-sex marriages ("Same sex marriage is destructive to Western civilization"), and in her fury against former President Clinton for defending the rights of lesbians to adopt children. "Talk about the power of ideology run amok!" cries Dr. Laura. "That the government permits a child to be robbed of a father to satisfy the political demands of gay activists is an outrage. Since when do people have a "right" to practice deviant sexual behavior and bring innocent children into their homes?"[27]

Again, the issue here is not whether Dr. Laura is right or wrong with regard to these matters. Many people are troubled by the legalization of same-sex marriages and the adoption of children by gay couples. What is significant is the intensity of Dr. Laura's *feelings* about these subjects. As if possessed of some deep fear that the order (Saturn) of the world is about to be irrevocably destroyed (Pluto), Dr. Laura sees herself as the last bastion of hope against a corrupt society.

Saturn, of course, symbolizes the father as the first and thus prototypical authority figure. It is tempting to speculate that Dr. Laura's allegation that the president has failed to protect children has its roots in her own father's failure to protect her—from *himself*. Recall that Schlessinger described her father as "verbally and physically abusive." Now, it is the government that is being abusive by default.

> If the welfare of our children is not the No. 1 priority, ideal and goal of this nation, then the nation will disintegrate. I talk to a lot of people in government, psychology and psychiatry every day who are afraid to stand up for the importance of the traditional family to the welfare of children....This has gone too far. We cannot continue to sacrifice our children on the altar of "freedom" and "diversity," no matter what the president of the United States proclaims.[28]

With an unintegrated Pluto-Saturn conjunction, there are two possibilities: either the government has failed to protect against evil, or is itself untrustworthy. Fear of the latter is evident in Dr. Laura's opposition to local government "head start" programs that provide compulsory pre-kindergarten for 3- and 4-year-olds.

Fearing the government will corrupt children's minds through "social retraining" and "sex education," Dr. Laura equates head start to George Orwell's novel *Animal Farm,* which is an allegory for a totalitarian state. "Any time a government entity tells parents that it knows more about the welfare of children than the caring, involved, nurturing and attentive mother and father, be afraid. Be VERY afraid." [29]

Her anger at the government's refusal to control the Internet is another example of a Saturn-Pluto wound. "There are obviously lots of reasons why our society — once so revered and respected around the world — is unraveling and degenerating," writes Dr. Laura. "But one of them is the unbridled license of communication on the Internet....The Internet is the most recent and most powerful tool to be commandeered by the sick evildoers in our midst. It spreads the virus of hate and germs of pathology like wildfire around the world, infecting more and more people, especially our neglected and vulnerable youth." [30]

Warning that the fabric of our society is being shredded by an abdication of responsibility (Saturn), she is "disgusted by the nonsense, the cowardice and the bad behavior of many politicians." As a nation we have become so desensitized to the immoral and the reprehensible, claims Dr. Laura, "that people who don't think sexual degradation and license are fun or funny are considered the villains in this country's unfolding immorality play." Schlessinger's wrath is not limited to the political sphere, but extends to the field of psychology as well. She believes that psychology as a discipline has propagated an amoral ethos. The normalization of homosexuality, liberalization of sexual practices, and excessive focus on self-esteem "have seriously damaged...our civilization," says Dr. Laura. [31]

While many people are in agreement with Dr. Laura's assessment of western civilization, I am more interested in the way she communicates her convictions. I suspect her impassioned rhetoric derives from a splitting of the wounded-healer (Pluto) archetype. There are two sides to every archetype. With Pluto, we have transformer-transformed, healer-wounded, doctor-patient, and wellness-sickness. Swiss analyst, Adolph Guggenbuhl-Craig, alleges that a splitting of the archetype occurs when the healer (doctor/therapist) projects her own wounds onto the patient and identifies solely with the wellness side. Yet, to the extent that she projects her inner patient onto the other, she becomes the charlatan—the dark side of the wounded-healer. The charlatan is operating when the healer tries to present herself as healthier (more pure and perfect) than she really is.

The same thing can happen with a Jupiter archetype, which likewise has two sides: moral-immoral, faith-doubt, and wisdom-ignorance. Just as the charlatan is a form of shadow that accompanies the healer, so the dark side of the guru is the hypocrite or false prophet. According to Guggenbuhl-Craig, doubt is the companion of faith, but no one wants to hear doubt expressed by a preacher. "Thus the priest often has no alternative but to be the hypocrite now and again, to hide his own doubts and to mask a momentary inner emptiness with high-flown words. If his character is weak, this can become a habitual stance."[32]

Like the clergyman, the therapist works with hunches and intuitions. Concepts and theories are the tools of her trade. Yet, there is great pressure to represent these tools as better than they really are and thus become possessed by the shadow—the charlatan or false prophet. When the therapist is trapped in the shadow of the false prophet she tries to allay her patient's need for guidance with a pretense of transcendental knowledge, e.g., Dr. Laura writes a book on *The Ten Commandments*. She hides her doubts and vulnerabilities behind a cloak of omnipotent omniscience. And because her patients embody qualities that she is loathe to admit in herself, they are threatening and must be subjugated. Accordingly, the charlatan-healer will evidence impatience, annoyance, and even hostility toward the very people she is pledged to help.

Power is inherent in the archetype of the wounded-healer. When the archetype is functioning in an integrated way, the healer has compassion for the wounded and is not afraid of the pain that their wound entails. There is an ability to recognize and identify with the patient's pain coupled with a wish to relieve it. The power to heal thus derives from a willingness to embrace the wound, to take it into oneself, as it were. However, if Pluto is not integrated, then there is fear and hostility toward what is perceived as a wholly objective evil. A polarity is set-up. On one side is the all-powerful, all-good healer; on the other side is the all-weak, all-bad patient.

This polarizing quality is clearly evident in Dr. Laura when she proclaims that our society is rapidly degenerating into a modern day Sodom and Gomorrah, whereas her values "are an oasis in the middle of a moral nothingness." Yet, she cannot truly have compassion for the pain of the wounded if their suffering reflects a condition that she has failed to face within herself. External power then becomes a substitute for internal power. Rather than embrace the wound, the shadow-healer seeks power *over* the feared thing. The intention is to subjugate or exterminate what, in fact, is actually a projected part of oneself. Shame, condemnation, and prosecution are a means to this end.

To the extent that Dr. Laura cannot admit that she is vulnerable to the same impulses and actions that afflict her callers, she has fallen prey to the shadow. If she perceives the Saturnian dimension of life as evil and corrupt, without recognizing that it is *her* Saturn that she is seeing, then she will project her wounds onto society and seek to resolve the crisis by attempting to gain power *over* the feared thing—e.g., over politicians, laws, rules and rule-makers.

If she sees an absence of responsibility, control, and regulation as the problem, then the solution is obvious: *more control and regulation.* Censor the Internet, forbid same sex marriages, legislate against abortion, punish, discipline, restrict!

In the eyes of many, Dr. Laura has become a kind of talk-show Dominatrix who dominates her callers in a weird, sadomasochistic relationship. The caller projects all his power onto Dr. Laura, and Dr. Laura projects all her badness onto the caller. Certainly, this would be consistent with an unintegrated Saturn-Pluto conjunction, which resembles nothing so much as a stern mommy who must "discipline" her bad children.

Salvadore Maddi, a professor of psychology and social behavior at the University of California, disapproves of Schlessinger's style. "Basically Dr. Laura is about: I'm right, everyone else is wrong. The hostility behind that is very tangible in the way she interacts with everyone. The more followers she gets, the more she's sure she's right. She needs very much to be in control."[33] Dr. Laura's followers are only too eager to hand over the reins. "A lot of people feel overwhelmed," Maddi explains. "People want there to be simple right-and-wrong answers: Spank me some more, Mama, and I'll do whatever you want!"[34]

CONCLUSION

Dr. Laura has stirred up a hurricane of protest that is raining down upon her with the vengeance of a biblical plague. What will be the result of this storm of public opinion? Many are hoping that Dr. Laura will simply dissolve, like the Wicked Witch of the West. She is not, after all, as the saying goes, a friend of Dorothy.

Regardless of what Dr. Laura thinks, no one is all good or all bad, including Dr. Laura. While the good that she accomplishes may be compromised by her faults and excesses, there can be no doubt that Schlessinger is frequently on the mark. More often than not her advice is sound and her intentions pure. If trouble and controversy continue to hound her, they will have been brought about by her failure to integrate the wounded-healer archetype. It matters little that Dr. Laura has admitted to behaviors that she has "shame and regret for." Evidence of a flourishing shadow is to be found not so much in her positions, with which many good people agree, but in her attitude. It is the anger, hostility, and arrogance behind her words that most disturbs.

Of course, everyone has a right to an opinion. Dr. Laura may be part of a conservative backlash that has real legitimacy. Yet, it is important to have tolerance for views that are different from one's own. Tolerance is not agreement or moral endorsement, for one can have compassion for behaviors that deviate from one's values without condoning those behaviors and placing them on the same moral plane as one's ideal.

Regrettably, Dr. Laura's shadow is entangled with precisely that which can be of help to others—her psychotherapeutic skills and religious faith. She uses these tools to weave about her an invisible cocoon that she hopes will shield her from pain and uncertainty. Thus rendered invulnerable, she never truly transforms but remains ensconced in her cocoon—a shrill, disembodied voice on the edge of a nation's conscience. Until and unless Dr. Laura integrates the shadow components of her birthchart, specifically her Yod to Uranus and her Saturn-Pluto conjunction, she will continue to polarize people because she is herself polarized. Healing requires a fundamental transformation of attitude toward that which one is striving to heal. Only through compassion—whether for her callers or society at large—can she hope to win over the forces that are arrayed against her.

Chapter Three

Astrology as Personal Mythology

AN EXAMINATION OF STAR WARS AND GEORGE LUCAS

I n this article, we will examine how the struggles of Luke Sky-walker and friends are little different from the struggles of George Lucas, author and creator of the six-part film series, *Star Wars*. In fact, each character of *Star Wars* can be seen to embody an aspect of Lucas' own personality as revealed by his astrological chart. More to the point, the conflicts between characters in *Star Wars* symbolize the intrapsychic conflicts of George Lucas.

Astrology has its roots in mythology. The mythological symbols we call signs and planets are the gods within that form the relationships of our psychic life. Planetary relations constitute psychodynamics—the movement and distribution of energies within the psyche. Not only do the structural dynamics of the psyche account for our outward behavior, they shape our artistic creations as well. That which is created is a metaphor of the consciousness from whence it springs.

The *Star Wars* trilogy has an epic, mythological quality, as if emerging from deep within the collective psyche. Because it touches upon needs and aspirations common to humanity, Jung would call such films *archetypal*. By now it's almost legendary that Lucas purposefully set out to refashion ancient myths for modern audiences. He was reading a lot of Joseph Campbell when he penned the script for *Star Wars*. Yet, while these films have universal significance, they also have a personal significance for George Lucas.

"Myths are public dreams," wrote Joseph Campbell, "and dreams are personal myths." Just as myths are symbolic of the collective life of humankind, so dreams are symbolic of the personal life of the individual. And dreams, or fantasy, are the stuff of which films are made. *Star Wars* is a case in point. The gods within George Lucas take their form in the heroes and villains of his films, battling across the galaxy in a grand homage to their creator, Lucas himself. In this sense, Lucas' "space fantasies" are actually self-portraits, metaphorical expressions of a rich and complex personal life. By making his dreams public, and in so doing creating a new, contemporary mythology, Lucas has unwittingly exposed the bare bones of his own psyche.

CHARTS ARE STORIES

An astrological chart can be thought of as a personal narrative, or life-story. Just as the planets and their various relations symbolize one's character, so they also symbolize the **plot** of one's story. Plot structure, therefore, is analogous to character structure. In a good story, all the elements are functionally related to each other. Plot structure is the arrangement of materials to give a single effect. The same holds true for the astrological chart, which is an arrangement of archetypes to have a particular effect, i.e., a fate or destiny. Each planetary character represents a type of action. Taken as a whole, the chart symbolizes the structure of action, *which is the plot of the story*. In other words, chart structure is made up of processes—aspects and dispositorships—that combine to create a larger, more encompassing pattern.

Planetary aspects symbolize the various types of relations—some conflictual, some harmonizing—that exist between parts of psychological structure. An aspect can be thought of as a kind of idea, or mythogem (mythic theme), that emerges out of the relative integration of the planets that make up the aspect. The linking of planets via aspects creates higher-level cognitive structures that tie processes together. Cognitive structures—ideas—predict the likelihood of the individual being able to meet the needs that each planet signifies. The aspect also symbolizes the strategy, or schema, for meeting these needs. For example, if Mars conjuncts Venus, the individual may believe in love at first sight and that intimacy is best attained through bold, decisive action.

> Where both are deliberate, the love is slight:
> Who ever loved, that loved not at first sight?*

FATE IS SOUL SPREAD OUT IN TIME

Like any good story, an astrological chart has a **pattern**; incidents of the same or similar quality keep reoccurring, e.g., an individual continually experiences the same kind of outcomes in his relationships, career, or finances. Ideally, pattern is not simply repetition, but constitutes a path of evolutionary unfoldment. Each incident modifies awareness, which leads toward a progressive development and integration of character. Every new episode has the potential to alter consciousness. People learn, develop insight, and realize their potentials over time. In this sense, plot is an unfolding of character; fate is soul spread out in time. One could even say that fate is the means whereby soul unifies itself.

As the action unfolds, there are invariably conflicts and allegiances that form between the various characters that make

---

* Christopher Marlowe (1564–1593), English dramatist, poet. *Hero and Leander,* "First Sestiad."

up the narrative. As archetypal characters, planets symbolize specific types of action, and every action has the potential for harmonizing or conflicting with other types of action. In other words, planetary characters have relations with one another for good or ill. The challenge of any story is to resolve conflicts and pull all the characters together into a harmonious whole. To the extent this is accomplished, one attains *character*, i.e. integrity and honor.

Conflict is essential to stories. This is as true for the average person as it is for the protagonists of myth and literature. Conflict is what drives a story forward. No conflict, no story. In external conflict, characters struggle against the environment or with each other. In internal conflict, one part of the psyche struggles against another part; motives clash and ideas vie for dominance. In most stories, a strong element of inner conflict balances the outer conflict. To understand a story it is crucial to determine the nature of the conflict and the pattern that the opposing forces assume. Toward this end the astrological chart is an invaluable aid, for almost invariably there is a central conflict clearly revealed in the horoscope. Often, there is more than one. Each conflict constitutes a kind of sub-plot within the overall story structure.

Aspects not only signify the organization of the internal world, they also describe how the external world is structured. Planetary archetypes are non-local entities that manifest simultaneously in both inner and outer events. Just as in stories, inner conflicts tend to be balanced by outer conflicts.

In the beginning of a story, there is generally some situation that entails a lack of wholeness—in other words, a conflict between characters, within a character, or both. Stories can be thought of in terms of problem and solution, conflict and repose, tension and resolution. Whether and how the conflict is resolved constitutes the main question of the drama. This is what creates suspense. A story is a movement through disunity to unity, complication to simplicity, mystery to revelation.

Again, a story can be seen as a metaphor for a person. Just as stories denote conflicts between characters, so every individual experiences internal conflict between the various parts of his own nature. The planetary archetypes make up our inner cast of characters. They are the gods and goddesses within that constitute the ongoing unfoldment of our psychic life. One part of our nature may be quite compatible with another part, e.g., our maternal instinct (Moon) may form an alliance (conjunction) with our inner warrior (Mars) so that we become fierce in our capacity to care and protect. Conversely, other parts of the psyche may be at war, e.g., our impulse for pleasure (Venus) may be at odds (opposition) with the drive for perfection (Saturn) so that we feel undeserving of pleasure. This may show up in the outer world as an interpersonal conflict. One person craves the pleasures of physical intimacy, the other withholds. The outer conflict reflects the inner one while also providing a vehicle for its resolution.

Purely physical conflict does not denote a story. A story requires characterization. There has to be characters that arouse sympathy or antipathy. We have to evaluate the ideas or motives that underlay the external conflict. We may sympathize with one character's perspective, and feel hostile toward another. Sympathy and antipathy, a conflict of ideas, is what makes up the story.

In astrology, too, the horoscope reveals how the native may be more sympathetic toward some planets than others.* Conflicting emotions and motivations can easily be portrayed by planetary aspects, e.g., the antagonism between family ties and personal inclination (Moon-Mars), friction between the individual and society (Mars-Venus), disharmony between the aesthetic and the

---

* The "native" is the person for whom the chart is cast.

practical sides of life (Venus-Saturn), dissonance between work and play (Saturn-Sun), and strife between career and family (Saturn-Moon).

Conflicts of motive are typically revealed in hard angles between planets, which often emerge as pathogenic beliefs—negative ideas—that express pessimism or fear about the relative likelihood of meeting basic needs. Negative ideas generate self-defeating behaviors that result in external conflicts and frustration of needs, and so the story goes.

The relation between character and events is a fundamental principle of organization in astrology, just as it is in stories. In story, plot is the unfolding of character; in astrology, character is destiny. Just as in every story there is an obvious external conflict and a less obvious internal conflict in the hero's mind, so each planetary aspect has an objective and subjective meaning. An aspect symbolizes a facet of character and a characteristic event.

If an individual believes that he can never truly belong (Moon) unless he achieves distinction in his profession (Saturn), while also fearing that too much work will jeopardize his relations with his family, this internal conflict of Moon-Saturn ideas may emerge externally, for example, as a situation in which his wife accuses him of neglecting the children in favor of his career. Often these conflicts appear as impossible predicaments for which there is no apparent solution. Yet, it is the challenge of the life to integrate the respective planetary functions and, in so doing, bring into being a unique talent or accomplishment that resolves the conflict. Perhaps he builds a company (Saturn) that provides a protective service (Moon) to the community, an accomplishment that ultimately allows him to spend more time with his family.

In every story, there is a key moment that brings into focus all previous events and suddenly reveals their meaning. It is the moment of **illumination** for the whole story, the instant in which the underlying unity is perceived as inherent in the complexity. All the relationships between the elements become clear and the story is seen to have a meaning as a whole. This meaning constitutes the story's key **theme**, which is the principle topic of the story. The moment of illumination also reveals the story's message or **moral**. Generally, this involves some lesson that the main character has to learn. A story's moral is revealed only after there has been a clear resolution or outcome of the main conflict.

Likewise in an astrological chart, there is a potential unity that is inherent in the complexity of the various parts and relations. If the chart is properly interpreted, this wholeness can be illumined. Suddenly the native sees his life as all of a piece; there is an "ah ha!" recognition. Most importantly, the native realizes that the main conflict of his life provides an opportunity for learning a lesson and for actualizing a potential that can only be achieved by working *through* complexity, complication, and confusion—just as in any good story. Pointing the way toward such a "happy ending" is one of the main values of interpreting a chart.

CONFLICT IN GEORGE LUCAS

By way of example, George Lucas, the creator and author of the *Star Wars* trilogy, has his Moon in Aquarius in the 10th opposing Pluto in Leo in the 4th (see Figure 5, p. 90). While it is not possible here to give a full interpretation of Lucas' chart, suffice to say this aspect represents one of the key themes in the Star Wars movies. One might argue that *Star Wars* is just fiction, just a story. But the point is that *every* life is a story, including the life of George Lucas. His Moon-Pluto opposition not only shows up in his fantasy life, it is alive and well in his "real" life, too. If everything is a metaphor of deeper, archetypal forces, it doesn't matter if we analyze Lucas' films or his own, personal experiences. The same

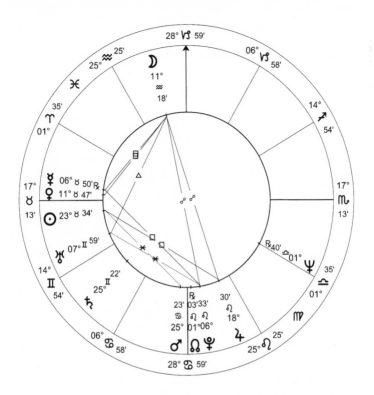

Figure 5: George Lucas, May 14, 1944, 5:40 am, Modesto, CA.

archetypal patterns will be there. Suffice to say that "Luke" is an equivalent for "Lucas." Symbolically speaking, the *Star Wars* trilogy is autobiographical.

The Moon, of course, symbolizes one's feelings and dependency needs; it is our capacity for tender, loving relations. It represents the feminine component of the male psyche. The Moon also signifies our experiences with mother, home and family. Pluto, on the other hand, symbolizes one's capacity for transformation through encounters with the shadow, evil, and death. The archetype of the wounded healer is Pluto's role.

When these two planets are in opposition, there is a potential conflict between the functions they symbolize. This often means that the Moon, the feminine, is "killed off" by Pluto, at least initially. One's capacity to love is wounded; feelings and dependency needs are repressed. Ultimately, this is what needs to be healed. To the extent that healing occurs, the individual's capacity to love is powerful indeed. Feelings are potent and deep, and one is able to penetrate others emotionally in a manner that is transformative.

Since Lucas' Moon is in the 10th, and the 10th house signifies father, we can assume that the injury is to the feminine component of the father's psyche, i.e., *father is wounded in his feeling function.* Since Pluto darkens the 4th house, which represents home and family, we can also assume that the problem originated in some crisis, or wounding, to the family. The Moon-Pluto opposition between the 4th and 10th suggests that the native's career (10th) requires him to regenerate a sense of family by healing his capacity to love. Also, he must attain mastery of his emotions and become a protector of the public. This, in effect, is his destiny.

In the beginning of one's life the core conflict in one's chart is generally at its most disintegrated state. We could speculate that Lucas' Moon-Pluto opposition initially manifested as some sort of loyalty conflict between his mother (4th house) and father (10th house). In other words, loving one parent might be perceived as damaging to the other. Also, an unintegrated Moon-Pluto opposition can signify a fear of being controlled, dominated, or devoured by a caring other. In Lucas' chart, this "caring other" could be mother and/or father, since both parents are implicated by virtue of the houses that are tenanted.* This would make lunar needs for belonging and closeness particularly problematic. For

---

* A planet in a house is said to "tenant" that house.

example, there may be a fear of never being able to separate from the family, as when a parent appropriates a child for his/her own needs. All of this could lead to repression of the lunar function. Young George Lucas might have found it dangerous to depend on others, trust his feelings, or allow himself to be emotionally close or vulnerable.

THE REAL STORY

There is an abundance of evidence in Lucas' life that testifies to the Moon-Pluto struggle. People who know him have always insisted that the tortured relationship between Darth Vader and Luke Skywalker springs, in many ways, from Lucas' relationship with his own father. George Sr. was a domineering, ultra right-wing businessman who every summer would shave off his son's hair and call him "Butch." Lucas recalls being "incredibly angry" at his father. They had raging arguments over young George's decision not to take over the family stationary business. Even after his son became extraordinarily wealthy, the elder Lucas, while proud, seemed surprised. He never believed his son would succeed at something of his own choosing.

A serious rupture occurred when Lucas went off to Hollywood instead of enlisting in the family stationary store. The elder Lucas tried everything to stop him. "I fought him; I didn't want him to go into that damn movie business," he told *Time* in 1983. "But George never listened to me. He was his mother's pet."[1] This is an interesting statement in that it suggests that the younger Lucas experienced his father's needs for him as too intense. It might also imply that his relationship with his mother was too close. There is at least the suggestion here of two Moon-Pluto themes: (1) a devouring parent (father and/or mother), and (2) closeness with the mother is hurtful to the father.

Lucas admits that his relationship with his father was strained, especially when he refused to go into the family business (Moon in 10th). "My father wrote me off," Lucas confesses, "he thought I wasn't going to amount to anything."[2] Lucas' father regarded George as an irresponsible dreamer destined for failure. "George was hard to understand," complained George Sr., "He was always dreaming things up."

Difficulty with authority was evident in high school as well. Lucas was a rebellious student with abysmally low grades. His teachers allowed him to graduate only because they thought George was going to die following a serious car accident just before school ended in his senior year. But Lucas fooled his teachers and survived. Later, at U.S.C. film school, he constantly broke rules and challenged the authority of his teachers. Lucas is famous for his hostility toward Hollywood executives, bankers and lawyers— anyone with control over him. After making his first commercial film, *THX 1138,* the filmmaker was infuriated over the "final cut" prerogative of studio executives who had the power to edit and change his film any way they pleased. Again, there is the theme of an intrusive authority (the studio executive) that tries to appropriate George for his own ends.

Lucas' fear of being controlled by studio heads prompted him to break with the industry and set up Zoetrope Studios in San Francisco with Francis Ford Coppola in the late 60's, thus repeating the theme of pushing away the father. The Hollywood grapevine immediately characterized them both as rebels and renegades. "We are the pigs," Lucas ranted in a 1979 interview, "you [Hollywood] can put us on a leash, keep us under control, but we are the guys who dig out the gold."[3] This statement is telling in light of the fact that Pluto often manifests as a fear of being dominated. Pluto also rules underground riches as in "we are the guys who dig out the gold."

THE LEO-AQUARIUS THEME

While the underlying issue is a Moon-Pluto one, it revolves around themes that pertain to Leo and Aquarius, the two signs that are involved in the opposition. Leo, of course, signifies the need for creative self-expression, while Aquarius pertains to themes of progress, change, technological innovation, revolution, and liberation (independence). On a more mundane level, Aquarius deals with the products and the means to change, e.g., science, advanced technology, and computers. With Moon Aquarius in the 10th, we can expect to see Aquarian themes played out in his career and in his relationships with authority. For example, it might manifest as an emotional need to break free from the conventions of the past and move toward a broader and more inclusive sense of family (Moon). Family could mean friends of like mind bound together for a common cause (Aquarius), such as the liberation of the masses from authoritarian repression (10th house).

Lucas admits, "there was a lot of rebellion when we came to San Francisco. We moved here in 1961 when I was 23 years old. We thought we were going to change the world."[4] A decade later, when Lucas set out to create Skywalker Ranch and his innovative special effects unit, Industrial Light and Magic, nervous Hollywood executives portrayed him as a cunning maverick bent on developing an independent empire to compete with—or even supplant—the major studios. Clearly, the themes of rebellion, innovation, and liberation were already apparent. Lucas' ruling passion was to wrench filmmaking from out of the grip of the past. "The old film studios have never been interested in research and science," complained Lucas in 1980. "We are nearing the 21st century, yet filmmaking is still very crude."[5]

It was Lucas' desire for control—or, perhaps more accurately, the fear of being controlled, that compelled him to establish an independent film research center in Marin County, CA. There, 425 miles north of Hollywood, tucked away in a bucolic valley hidden from view, Lucas and his band of rebels—his Moon Aquarius family—built Skywalker Ranch and collaborated in new techniques of filmmaking. At Lucasfilm and Industrial Light and Magic in San Rafael, Lucas built what is considered the most technically advanced filmmaking enterprise in the world. Having spearheaded a revolution in the technology and employment of special effects, and having ushered in a whole new era for science fiction, Lucas has indeed changed the world of filmmaking. Again, we see how home and family (Moon) combines with the urge to reform (Aquarius) in the context of career (10th house).

INTEGRATION

The integration of the Moon-Pluto opposition is evident in the way Lucas has come to terms with his own dark side, i.e., his fear of dependency and his resentment of authority, and how this, in turn, has brought about reconciliation with his family. Recall that initially Lucas seemed reluctant to do anything but rebel against authority figures. His father worried that he was a dreamer and lacked ambition; Lucas saw his father as suffocating and controlling. It was only by confronting death (Pluto) in the hospital following his accident that Lucas found the incentive to begin his professional career.

After 48 hours in a coma and weeks in intensive care, Lucas' brush with death changed his life. "It was a rite of passage. I felt, now that I have a second chance, I'm going to make the most of it."[6] The accident, Lucas added, gave him a sense of his own mortality and put him in touch with his *feelings*. "I began to trust my instincts," he said. "I had the feeling I should go to college, and I did. I had the same feeling later that I should go to film school, even though everyone thought I was nuts. I had the same feeling when I decided to make *Star Wars*, when even my friends told me I was crazy."[7] Here we see the close relationship between Pluto (death) and the Moon (feelings). Only after facing death was he able to fully open to his feelings.

Following his recovery, he continued to battle authority throughout his college and early professional life. Yet, with the unprecedented success of *Star Wars*, Lucas became the absolute authority he so feared and resented in others. Jung would call this *enantiodromia,* the tendency for things to revert to their opposites. Lucas admits, "I was a control freak."[8] His colleagues agree. "I think what drives him as a businessman is control," says Rick McCallum, the producer of the *Star Wars* special editions. "Control over his work. That's primary."[9] A former attorney of Lucas', Tom Pollock, reveals that he didn't really understand George until he met his father and talked with the elder Lucas about his son. The similarities were startling. "That's when I realized," said Pollock, "George *is* his father."[10]

At his Skywalker Ranch film studio, Lucas is in supreme command. Now it is *he* who makes "final cut" and influences corporate policy in Hollywood. By establishing a home base from which he can work in his own way (Moon in Aquarius in the 10th), Lucas wields a power greater than that previously projected onto superiors. No longer evil, or something to resist, Lucas has integrated the thing he most feared in himself—his own 10th house authority. His success as a filmmaker also allowed him to make peace with his father. "Now he's proud of me," Lucas stated in 1980, "the fact that I actually went to college and am successful at what I do."[11]

Conflict In Star Wars

It is worth noting that Lucas and his band of rebels at Skywalker Ranch bear a startling resemblance to the Rebel Alliance in *Star*

Wars. First, Lucas had to revolt against his father who sought to appropriate him into the family business, just as Luke Skywalker had to resist Darth Vader's attempts to seduce him into the dark side of the Force. Second, Lucas revolted against the rigid corporate structure of Hollywood and won the freedom to make films his own way. Likewise, a key theme in *Star Wars* involves "freedom fighters"—the Rebel Alliance—that struggle to liberate themselves from the emperor's oppressive control.

In effect, the characters in *Star Wars* recapitulate the struggles and aspirations of Lucas' actual life. The themes of his films and the events of his life are metaphorical equivalents. Both are expressions of conflicting forces in his psyche. Lucas himself confesses the similarity. "A lot of stuff in there is very personal," he said years after *Star Wars* was released. "There's more of me in *Star Wars* than I care to admit."[12]

Recall that a major theme of a Moon-Pluto opposition involves a wound to the feminine function. The need for belonging and closeness is in conflict with the need for transformation and power. With Pluto, whatever needs to be transformed is by definition wounded; thus, very likely there has been some kind of trauma to the lunar function. This suggests that the Moon may be repressed and associated with suffering. Expression of dependency may stimulate a memory of being overpowered, exploited, or violated. Hence all things related to the Moon—family, emotional vulnerability, tenderness, and caring—have been abducted by Pluto into the underworld of the soul. This is the hidden source of shame and pain, the "dark secret" that needs to be redeemed.

In an opposition, each planet is the other's open enemy or partner, depending upon the degree of integration. To the extent that the opposition remains unintegrated, each planet regards the other with animosity, e.g., Lucas' need for closeness (Moon) triggers a perception that the world "out there" is exploitive, evil, or emotionally devouring (Pluto)—especially figures that are associated with the houses tenanted, i.e., father and authority figures (10th), or family and caretakers (4th). However, if the opposition is integrated, then one's capacity for caring and healing are joined in matrimony, so to speak. Feelings run deep and there is an ability to regenerate in others a capacity to love. This occurs by penetrating the other's emotional defenses, containing their pain, and loving in them precisely those places where they are wounded and ashamed. In other words, one transforms the other through an act of caring. But first one must heal oneself.

A planet in a house symbolizes both an inner and an outer reality. Accordingly, since the opposition occurs between the 4th and 10th houses, we can assume that 10th house figures, beginning with the father, are potentially wounded in their feeling function; i.e., the feminine component of the father's psyche is damaged. Likewise, with Pluto in the 4th *and* opposing the Moon, this is a signature of double jeopardy in the family. There is likely to be something dark here, some condition that is shameful, frightening, and in need of redemption. To the extent that the lunar wound in the 10th is healed, Lucas will resolve his distrust of authority and become a source of love, support, and protection for families within the public domain, i.e., his career is characterized by a capacity for caring that is regenerative. He becomes the master not of disaster, but of family empowerment.

In *Star Wars*, we immediately see evidence of a lunar wound in Luke Skywalker, who is introduced as an orphan living with his aunt and uncle on a dry, inhospitable planet infested with dangerous, dark creatures—sandpeople—lurking in shadows. Luke yearns to separate from his adoptive parents and join the academy to become a pilot, but his uncle insists that he stay on the farm to work for another year. Luke feels trapped and exploited.

By the end of the first act, his aunt and uncle are roasted by the Imperial stormtroopers. We eventually learn that Luke's father has been transformed into the evil Darth Vader, his mother is dead, and his sister, Leia, is a princess yet unknown to him. The family, in short, has been destroyed. Throughout most of this first film, Luke is emotionally upset, angry, and impatient with people around him. He is warned not to give in to the Dark Side, which feeds off negative feelings—fear, hatred, anger, and revenge.

At this point in the story, Luke embodies an unintegrated Moon-Pluto opposition. Obi Wan Kenobi cautions him, "Don't give in to hate or anger; they lead the way to the Dark Side." The message is clear: certain kinds of feelings are dangerous; you must learn to integrate and control them or they will possess you and turn you into an evil thing, as they did Darth Vader.

Vader, too, embodies an unintegrated version of Moon-Pluto. His pain mirrors Luke's. In fact, Luke and Vader represent two poles of the opposition. Both are equally unintegrated at the beginning of the film. As 10th house authority in the empire, Vader is singularly evil. He represents the Dark Side of the Force, "the quick and easy way," and has a ruthless and seductive power that appears invincible. Cloaked in black robes and body armor, a mechanical monster stripped of his humanity, his true self remains hidden, a dark secret beneath flickering lights and an artificial respirator that keeps him alive. He hasn't even a face to betray a glimmer of kindness. Here we have the perfect symbol of Moon in the 10th opposed Pluto; Darth Vader is "Dark Father," a powerful man who is wounded in his feminine side. He seems devoid of any capacity for feeling or caring. Recall that Vader's mission is to subjugate the rebel planets of the empire into a single *family*—albeit, a family that is controlled through force and intimidation. This itself is a grim expression of the devouring mother, the caretaker that would sooner kill you than allow you to separate from her lethal embrace.

Luke Skywalker, on the other hand, is the wounded Moonchild, seeking to recover that which he lost long ago—a home and family free from the evil and tyranny that Vader symbolizes. The Moon-Pluto conflict heightens when Yoda tests Luke by having him enter a cave "strong with the Dark Side of the Force." Shivering with apprehension, Luke asks, "What's in there?" "Only what you bring with you," is Yoda's cryptic reply. Luke descends into the cave and immediately we see symbols of Pluto—a damp dark underworld inhabited by slithering snakes and assorted reptiles. He moves deeper into the cave and suddenly Darth Vader emerges out of the shadows. In a dream-like sequence, Luke engages in a light sword duel with his enemy, whom he decapitates. Vader's mask breaks away and reveals Luke's own face. Later, when he battles the real Vader, we are able to understand the apparition. Just as Luke is about to be slain by the Dark Lord, Vader tells him with horrifying certainty, "I am your father," and tempts Luke to join with him and the Dark Side of the Force.

In both sequences it is suggested that the evil that Vader symbolizes is in Luke as well. For Luke to confront Vader is to confront his own dark side—the hatred within that compels him to avenge the destruction of his family. The fact that Vader is Luke's own father again symbolizes that Luke's conflict is an internal one; it is the Vader within that he must slay.

It is interesting to note that it is only through "trusting his feelings" that Luke is able to open himself to the power of the Force. As a symbol of the wounded part of the psyche, Pluto signifies that which we distrust. Whatever it touches, especially by hard aspect, takes on the quality of something dark and forbidden. It is both the wound within the psyche, and the healer of the wound. Its message is simple but never easy: you must die; you must confront your darkness, slay your dragon and be reborn anew.

The Moon, on the other hand, signifies one's feelings and capacity to depend on a loving other. It is only through the integration of these two faculties—Moon *and* Pluto—that Luke is able to trust his feelings and thereby ally himself with the Light Side of the Force. In other words, Luke's real mission is to learn how to contain and ultimately transform the negative feelings that threaten to possess him. To the extent that his identity is predicated upon repression of these feelings, he must *die* to his old self. For his true self can only be restored by integrating that which he fears—his pain and shame. He must learn to accept that Vader *is* his father, but that love is more powerful than hate. He must learn to depend on the Force and regenerate his capacity to love. Only then will he be empowered on an emotional level.

Integration of the Moon-Pluto opposition is prefigured in the characters of Obi-Wan Kenobi and Yoda, two Jedi masters that serve as adoptive parents to Luke, training him in the art of feeling. Over and again he is told to relax, turn inwards, and feel the Force flowing within him. Their love and support provide Luke with a kind of corrective emotional experience that enables him to eventually confront his shadow, personified by Vader.

THE KEY MOMENT

In each of the three original Star Wars films—*Star Wars, The Empire Strikes Back,* and *Return of The Jedi*—there is a key moment when the Moon-Pluto theme is fully revealed. Near the end of *Star Wars,* Luke is encouraged by the discarnate voice of his mentor, Obi-wan, to *trust his feelings* precisely when he is required to shoot the lethal rocket into the interior of the Death Star. But, to trust his feelings he has to *depend* on the Force, which is the supreme intelligence and power of the Universe. "Let go, Luke," says Obi Wan, "Trust the Force." Luke turns off his computerized targeter, closes his eyes, turns inward and shoots his missile. It penetrates the one vulnerable spot on the Death Star and blows it to bits.

In the sequel, *The Empire Strikes Back,* the key moment is when Luke is told by Darth Vader, "*I* am your father. Search your feelings; you know it to be true. Join with me and together we can rule the galaxy as father and son." Again he is required to trust his feelings in a dangerous situation; he could be seduced by his paternal longings into the Dark Side. Again Luke has to "let go," this time to tumble head over foot into the empty abyss of the reactor shaft in a desperate attempt to escape Vader's hypnotic power. When the Moon opposes Pluto, trusting one's feelings can literally feel like falling into a deep, black hole—a motif that occurs again and again in Lucas' films.*

Finally, in *Return of The Jedi,* the key moment occurs when Vader "turns" and rescues Luke from the evil Emperor. Earlier, Luke told Vader, "I will not turn—you will be forced to destroy me....Search your feelings, Father. You can't do this. I feel the conflict within you. Let go of your hate." This time it is Vader who must "let go." Vader emerges as the film's ultimate hero when he realizes that Luke is right; love *is* stronger than hate. And with this realization he forthwith dispatches the Emperor by throwing him into the reactor shaft where he is annihilated in a fitting, plutonic explosion. Although this heroic act ultimately kills Vader, he has already been healed and transformed by his son's love. When Luke cries out to his father, "I've got to save you," Vader replies, "You

---

* The Moon-Pluto motif of the devouring mother occurs in a variety of guises throughout the *Star Wars* trilogy, as well as in all the Indiana Jones films (also by Lucas). For example, in *Star Wars* there is the garbage compactor on the Death Star, replete with a devouring dragon that pulls Luke down below the surface of the foul water. Then the compactor walls begin to close in on Luke, Han, and Leia. In *The Empire Strikes Back*, Luke plummets down the reactor shaft toward what seems certain death. Also, Han Solo flies the Millennium Falcon into a cave that turns out to be the open mouth of a monstrous Jonah-like creature. In *Return of the Jedi* there is the underground lair of the Bantha monster who nearly swallows Luke, and again, later, there is the Sarlacc creature in the desert that is a virtual hole in the ground with teeth and tentacles that reach up and pull unwilling victims into its belly where they are "digested over a thousand years." All of these images attest to Lucas's preoccupation with being devoured by large, powerful entities that are symbolic of a devouring womb/mother that will not permit separation.

already have, Luke." And in his final moment, he whispers: "Luke, you were right...you were right about me...Tell your sister...you were right."

THE MOON-PLUTO THEME

In each of these three key moments, the Moon-Pluto theme is fully revealed. Both Luke and Vader had to open to their feelings, let go of control, and face the possibility of death. In so doing, there was healing, transformation, and empowerment. One could argue that evil is born out of a failure to transform, to suffer pain, to die to one's old self and be reborn. The first trilogy reveals that this was Vader's original sin; it was *why* he became Vader. He could not tolerate —"let go"— to the pain (Pluto) of his emotions (Moon) when he lost his mother in an earlier episode of *Star Wars*. He did not trust that the way of healing is *through* death.

THE BACKGROUND OF THE STORY

In the retrospective episodes of I-III, we learn of Anakin Skywalker's early traumas that led to his eventual conversion into Darth Vader. Episode I, *The Phantom Menace,* reveals that nine-year-old Anakin, "Annie," was raised as a slave on the desert world of Tatooine with his slave mother, Shmi Skywalker. The cruel and oppressive slave master, Watto, owned both of them. Anakin never knew his father, and his mother would not reveal the father's identity when asked by Qui Gon, the Jedi Knight who discovered Anakin.

If the 4th house is one's family of origin, or "motherland," then the hot, hellish environs of Tatooine, inhabited by barbaric savages, ruthless criminals, and reptilian thugs who gamble on gladiatorial "pod" races, is an apt symbol for Pluto in Leo in the 4th. Pluto, of course, symbolizes the underworld, which psychologically represents the shadow—the dark and unknown side of the self that must eventually be integrated.

Again, not only is Pluto in the house of the Moon (the 4th), it's also *opposing* the Moon, thus repeating the Moon-Pluto theme. This suggests an injury to the feminine dimension of the self, a lunar-wound if you will. Anakin and his mother's disempowered, pain-filled, shame-ridden status on Tatooine depict the Moon-Pluto relationship quite clearly; it's a degeneration of the feminine that must ultimately be regenerated.

Psychologically, this aspect connotes an intense *fear* that one's lunar needs will not be fulfilled, that they are bad, and that expression of them makes one vulnerable to further pain and humiliation. In anticipation of this, the individual will generally try to gain control *over* that which is feared—rejection, neglect, or aloneness. This can range from emotionally manipulative, covert, or demanding behavior to *doing to the other what has been done to you.* In one manner or another, extreme measures are taken to avoid the pain that is associated with lunar needs for closeness and belonging.

It is significant that Anakin's dream to become a Jedi requires him to leave his mother. After learning that his mother could not be freed and would not be leaving Tatooine with him, Anakin was devastated.*

> Everything was coming apart inside, all the happiness melting away, all the expectancy fading. But then he felt his mother's hands tighten over his own, and in her touch he found the strength he needed to do what he knew he must....."I'm going to miss you so much," he whispered.[13]

And as he was leaving with Qui-Gon...

---

* In the novel, *Episode I: The Phantom Menace,* the full extent of this trauma was more fully explored than in the film, which omitted many significant scenes. Likewise, the novel, *Episode II: Attack of The Clones,* reveals much more of Anakin Skywalker's inner world. The remaining quotes in this section are taken from those two books, both of which are based on the story and screenplay by George Lucas.

He glanced back one more time at his mother. Seeing her standing in the doorway brought him about. He stood there momentarily, undecided, conflicting emotions tearing at him. Then his already shaky resolve collapsed altogether, and he raced back to her. By the time he reached her, he was crying freely. "I can't do it, Mom," he whispered, clinging to her. "I just can't!" He was shaking, wracked with sobs, disintegrating inside so quickly that all he could think about was holding on to her. Shmi let him so for a moment, comforting him with her warmth, then backed him away.[14]

Throughout the remainder of the novel, Anakin's pain over the loss of his mother is repeatedly mentioned. Moreover, he fears for her safety and feels guilty for leaving her behind. To separate from Shmi, he must learn to repress his feelings. His mother instructs him, "Now be brave, and don't look back." It is the beginning of a pattern that will ultimately have poisonous consequences, as is typical of an unintegrated Moon-Pluto opposition.

Qui-Gon assumes the role of Anakin's surrogate father and there is a genuine and growing love between them. Soon, however, Qui-Gon is dead, and Anakin's loss of his mother is exacerbated. Qui-Gon—Anakin's first real father figure—is killed in a light sword duel with the evil Darth Maul. Hence Anakin's satisfaction at becoming a Jedi is "clouded by the sadness he could not banish at losing Qui-Gon and his mother both". With the Jedi master's death, "Anakin was left adrift. There was no one who could give him the grounding that Qui-Gon had provided....he felt all alone...sick in spirit and lost in his heart."[15]

Anakin's only consolation is a fantasy that one day he will be a powerful enough to return to Tatooine and free his mother. This is his dream, his life plan. Psychologically, the fantasy of omnipotence compensates for the pain and impotence he feels as a child. Anakin and Shmi's status as slaves symbolize the disempowerment that is a frequent consequence of hard aspects between Moon and Pluto. Disempowerment permeates the ruptured emotional bond between mother and child; it is implicit in the shame and secrecy surrounding Anakin's real father, and it provides the underlying motivation for Anakin's obsession to become a Jedi, for only then would he have the power to free his mother and make his family whole again. "I will become a Jedi," he declared in a small voice. "And I will come back and free you, Mom. I promise."

In *Episode II: Attack of the Clones*, nineteen-year-old Anakin has grown into fledgling status as a Jedi apprentice. But he is headstrong and feels held back by Obi-Wan Kenobi, his Jedi master. Here again we see shades of Lucas feeling held back by his father. Late in the film, Anakin grows increasingly agitated by recurrent nightmares of his mother, whom he senses is in terrible pain. Returning to Tatooine, he discovers she has been abducted by Tuscan Raiders—primitive sand people—and may be dead. Sensing she is still alive, Anakin speeds off to rescue her.

In the novel, Shmi Skywalker is described as suffering terrible pain. Caked with blood, her ribs crushed, her swollen and battered body hanging from a rack where she has been bound and tortured by the Tuscan Raiders, she clings to life in hopes that Anakin will feel her love for him through the Force.

> She needed that, needed to complete the cycle, to let her son recognize that through it all, through the missing years and the great distances between them, she had loved him unconditionally and thought of him constantly....Without the memories of Annie and the hope that he would feel her love for him, she would surely have given up long ago and allowed herself to die.[16]

Indeed, Annie does find her, but it is too late. In the most moving moment of the film, Anakin steals into the Tuscan camp and cuts his way into his mother's tent. Shmi recognizes him and starts to tell him, "I love..." and then goes still. "She looked straight up, past Anakin, past the hole in the ceiling, to the shining Moon." Anakin becomes immobilized by the confusion and unreality of what is happening, and begins to feel "a budding rage and the most profound sense of emptiness he had ever known." He is wracked with guilt that he left his mother on Tatooine, that he couldn't free her, couldn't save her. Consumed with hatred and rage, he gives himself over to emotions that he knows are "of the dark side." Within minutes he has slaughtered everyone in the camp—men, women, and children. At the end of his rampage, "He didn't feel empty any longer. He felt a surge of energy and strength beyond anything he had ever known, felt full of the Force, full of power, full of life."[17]

Clearly, this is a turning point in the evolution of Anakin Skywalker's character. Although Padme (Anakin's future wife) tries to help Anakin grieve the loss of his mother, his pain and guilt is too much. Rather than open to the full reality of his loss and with it acceptance of his own limitations, Anakin compensates in the opposite direction. Padme gently reminds him that despite being a Jedi warrior, he doesn't have control over death. "You're not *all*-powerful," she says.

> He stiffened at her words and pulled away from her—and angrily, she realized. "But I should be!" he growled, and then he looked at her, his face a mask of grim determination. "And someday I will be!"
>
> "Anakin, don't say such things," Padme replied fearfully, but he didn't even seem to hear her.
>
> "I'll be the most powerful Jedi ever!" he railed on. "I promise you! I will even learn to stop people from dying!"[18]

This is the key moment of the film so far as revealing the beginning of Anakin's descent into darkness. His lunar wound is too great. He failed to free and save his mother, which was his primary reason for becoming a Jedi. The only meaning he could derive from this failure was that *he was not powerful enough.* Rather than honoring death and the inevitable pain that it brings in its wake, Anakin resolved to defeat death. It was only through his son—Luke Skywalker—that he ultimately realized his mistake. To heal his wound, Vader had to learn to open to his feelings no matter how grievously painful they might be. For healing is only possible by finding the courage to face death on an emotional level.

The murder of Anakin's mother, and more importantly his failure to save her, sets the stage for Episode III—*Revenge of the Sith*—wherein further emotional trauma overwhelms Anakin completely. His Jedi "family" require him to spy upon Supreme Chancellor Palpatine, who has assumed near dictatorial powers in the intergalactic senate. The Jedi Council regards Palpatine as a threat to freedom and democracy (Aquarius theme). Yet, the Chancellor has always been a kindly father figure to Anakin— gentle, protective, and emotionally sympathetic, the perfect image of Moon in the 10th. Underneath Palpatine's fatherly façade, however, lurks an evil Sith Lord—Darth Sidious—whose hidden agenda is to "turn" Anakin to the dark side of the Force. Again, the Moon's opposition to Pluto is in evidence, for Palpatine's tenderness toward Anakin harbors a wicked intent.

Anakin feels betrayed by his Jedi family, whom he knows do not fully trust him. Torn between his loyalty to the Chancellor and his duties as a Jedi, Anakin is like an emotional volcano about to erupt. His most troubling concern, however, lies with his beautiful wife, senator Padme Amidala. Secretly married at the end of Episode II (Jedi's are not allowed to form emotional attachments), they are deeply, hopelessly in love.

Padme is 9 years older than Anakin. Her character has evolved from surrogate mother in Episode I to forbidden lover in Episode III. Clearly, this represents the Moon-Venus square (woman as mother and as lover), and the Venus-Pluto square (love, intimacy and attachment associated with risk, danger, and taboo). Indeed, after discovering that Padme is pregnant with their child, Anakin has a terrifying premonition of her dying in childbirth. Palpatine psychically intuits this and exploits Anakin's fear by intimating that Sith Lords have the power to reverse death. Anakin is still tortured with the guilt and pain of not being able to save his mother; thus, he is absolutely determined not to lose his wife. Somehow he *will* find a way to save her. Anakin seeks guidance from the most powerful Jedi alive, *Yoda*.

"The fear of loss is a path to the dark side, young one," warns Yoda. "Rejoice for those who transform into the Force. Mourn them not. Miss them not. The shadow of greed, attachment is. What you fear to lose, train yourself to release. Let go of fear, and loss cannot harm you." In essence, Yoda is saying that loss, pain, and death are natural experiences for every human being. It is the inordinate fear of and wish to avoid such experiences that makes one vulnerable to the dark side.

If the Moon signifies our emotional attachments, and Venus our physical ones, and each is in hard aspect to Pluto, then attachment and the inevitability of death are at odds. Consistent with an unintegrated T-Square, Anakin ignores Yoda's advice and pits himself—the lunar and Venusian parts of himself—*against* death. This is the square and opposition to Pluto. Anakin is polarized to death, but not for long. Ultimately he comes to embody it so fully that his capacity to care (Moon) and to love (Venus) is nearly extinguished.

Once he discovers that Palpatine is Darth Sidious, and that he can teach Anakin how to reverse death, Anakin cannot allow the

Jedi to kill him. For Palpatine's death would mean the irretrievable loss of the very knowledge that would empower Anakin to restore Padme's life. Driven by his fear of loss, and compelled to gain power over death, Anakin commits the unpardonable sin of aiding Palpatine in the killing of a fellow Jedi, and so collapses fully into the dark side.

The story races to its conclusion when Anakin, now transformed into Darth Vader, is sent by Darth Sidious on a veritable killing spree that includes the extermination of younglings—Jedi children in training. Symbolically, this signifies the murder of Anakin's inner child, his own lunar nature, and with it the longings and fears that he could never quite contain. In the final, climactic scene on the burning, hellish planet of Mustufar, surrounded by rivers of molten lava, Padme confronts Anakin with allegations that he has turned to the dark side. He retorts, *"Everything* I have done, I have done for *you."* And then, upon discovering that Obi-Wan has accompanied her, Anakin uses the Force to strangle Padme in a fit of murderous rage.

In the lightsword duel with Obi-Wan that follows, Anakin's legs and arm are severed from his body, and his torso bursts into flames upon a molten shore of black glass sand. The symbolism, as always, is apt, for never was there a more perfect rendering of a Plutonic underworld than Mustufar with its exploding volcanoes and rivers of fire. Surely Anakin is in hell. Though Mustufar claims Anakin, it is not to be his final end, for Darth Sidious finds him and converts what remains of his body into the half-machine remnant that becomes the Darth Vader of Episodes IV-VI: black cape, mechanical arms and legs, optical and audio sensors, artificial respirator, and cold electrosonic voice.

The transformation is complete, but the story is not over. *Episode III – Revenge of the Sith,* is but a phase in the healing journey of the Skywalker family. The Moon-Pluto theme of this particular film is clear: emotional trauma can lead to an attempt to ward off painful feelings associated with death. Following the loss, torture, and murder of his mother, Anakin is portrayed as an emotionally intense, volatile young man with a limited capacity to control his darker feelings—fear, anger, impatience, jealousy, revenge, and aggression.

"Trust your feelings" is a refrain heard throughout the Star Wars saga, but this is precisely the point: if there is sufficient build-up of emotional pain, one's feelings can be overwhelming; thus, they are repressed. Once repressed, however, they build up even more pressure until, like a Mustufar volcano, they erupt from below and utterly possess the individual. Anakin's inability to accept the traumatic loss of his mother, and his subsequent fear of death, compel him to attempt the impossible: to defeat death itself so that he will no longer be vulnerable to its sting. Yet, in so doing, the love that he tries to save, he destroys; his very effort to avert Padme's death is what ultimately kills her.

With Moon-Pluto, it is not enough to simply trust one's feelings. They must be mastered, too. This is Anakin's failure. He cannot conquer his fears; thus, they conquer him, destroying his capacity for vulnerability and true love. By the end of Episode III, Anakin is emotionally "dead," having killed off his lunar and Venusian feelings. Yet, Padme's dying words presage *Episode IV – A New Hope*, "There...is still good in him," she whispers to Obi-Wan. "I know there is...still..."

That faith will come to be embodied in Luke Skywalker, Anakin's son, who is able to accomplish what his father could not: a full integration of the Moon-Venus-Pluto T-Square. Luke learns to control his darker feelings and retain his capacity to love even in the face of death. In *Star Wars*, Luke faced death when he trusted his feelings and attacked the menacing Death Star without his targeter; in *The Empire Strikes Back* he faced death when he resisted

Vader's seductive appeals and jumped into the reactor shaft; in *Return of the Jedi* he faced death when he refused to kill his father and become the Emperor's minion. And finally, it was Vader who faced death when his feelings "turned" and he threw the Emperor into the reactor shaft. While this act of love proved fatal, it was also self-redemptive, enabling Vader to be reborn as his true self—Anakin (and again) Skywalker—a play on words that tells us Vader was meant to be a Pluto symbol of death and rebirth. In healing his father, Luke substantiates his mother's claim, "There is still good in him."

A CONFLICT OF IDEAS

The *Star Wars* trilogy is also about a conflict of Moon-Pluto ideas. The pathogenic version of the aspect is: "You should not trust your tender feelings, nor should you depend on anyone, for love makes you weak and dark forces will exploit your emotional vulnerability. Therefore repress your pain; give in to your hatred, anger, and revenge, for these pave the way to true power."

Clearly, this idea is embodied in the character of Darth Vader, who literally masks his feelings under an ominous black mask and cloak. The healthy, integrated version is taught by Yoda and Obi-wan, and ultimately comes to be embodied in Luke: "Trust your feelings, open to your capacity to love even at great emotional risk, for the Force will then be with you." Here, the Force is the ultimate Moon-Pluto symbol, for it binds the Universe together, permeates and unifies all things, and can only be accessed by "letting go" of one's thoughts and intentions. This, of course, is how one accesses the Moon, by letting oneself be vulnerable, by turning inward and *feeling*.

The Moon-Pluto theme also contains the moral of the story. For Luke, the lesson he had to learn was to control his angry, bitter, and vindictive feelings and transform them into love, a love so powerful that it can penetrate the darkest evil, eliminate hatred, and heal a soul—that of his father. The moral of the story is "don't give up on the goodness in people; relate to the higher man, good and evil can be reconciled through love."

When Luke surrenders himself to Vader near the end of *Return of the Jedi*, his Moon-Pluto opposition is fully integrated. He addresses Vader as "Father" for the first time, and reminds him, "you were once Anakin Skywalker, my father....It is the name of your true self." Vader resists, but Luke's emotional power has already penetrated his father's defenses. "I know there is good [love] in you," he says, "that's why you could not destroy me." Vader acknowledges his son's ability—which is really the power of his love—when he responds, "Indeed, you *are* as powerful as the Emperor has foreseen." Although the Dark Lord tries to resist, his emotions are moved. That Luke has touched his father's feelings is evidenced by Vader's final statement in the scene, "It is too late for me, Son." One senses Vader's anguish when he has to steady himself against the railing as Luke is taken away. He has resisted Luke for the moment, but it is only a matter of time before he turns completely, i.e., transforms.

In *Star Wars,* the Moon-Pluto theme is at its most disintegrated state. Luke's family (Moon) has been destroyed and evil (Pluto) reigns. Significantly, it was a woman (Moon) in danger (Pluto) that ignites Luke's healing journey, for it was his familial love for Leia, his sister, that inspires him to seek out Obi-wan. Again, the main conflict revolves around Moon and Pluto. Will Luke's family/Moon be reunited, or completely annihilated? Will Luke be turned by the Emperor to the Dark Side of the Force, or will he succeed in killing or perhaps even turning Vader to the Light Side—healing Vader's feminine wound? Luke's willingness to complete his training, a kind of martial arts therapy with Yoda, readies him for the final confrontation with Vader and his own dark side. He does *not* turn; he would rather die (Pluto) than give in to hatred, kill his father, and become the Emperor's pawn.

This is the moment of illumination in *Episode VI: Return of the Jedi*. Luke foils the Emperor's plans, and darkness is transformed into light when Vader throws the Emperor into the reactor shaft where he explodes in a brilliant flash. In that moment, father and son are reunited. Shortly after, when the missile penetrates the Death Star's main reactor, there is again a brilliant explosion, like a fulminant supernova. These are all metaphors of lunar transformation. The Death Star was a dark, evil womb (another Moon-Pluto image) that contained at its atomic core the heart of evil itself, the Emperor. The sole purpose of the Death Star was to hold the planets in place and never let them become independent, self-governing entities.

Whereas in *Star Wars* we witnessed the Death Star shatter Leia's home planet into a billion pieces, by the end of *Return of the Jedi* it is the Death Star that is annihilated. Disunity has been reconciled into a new Moon-Pluto unity. By working through complexity, complication, and confusion, Luke fulfilled his destiny as an emotional master; he transformed hate into love, healed his father, and regenerated his family, newly composed of Han, Leia, Chewbacca, the children (Ewoks and Droids) and the ancestors—Yoda, Obi Wan, and Anakin Skywalker. Wholeness has returned. Order again prevails in the Universe.

SUMMARY AND DISCUSSION

Lucas' *Star Wars* trilogy exemplifies how a single aspect can be a powerful thematic element in a life story. The main psychological conflict within Luke Skywalker, which was mirrored by an interpersonal conflict with his father, was clearly symbolized by the Moon-Pluto opposition. This same aspect also represented the story's primary theme, the core conflict of ideas, the key moment of illumination, and the moral lesson imparted.

In every instance, there is a clear parallel with George Lucas' personal life. At the beginning of *Star Wars*, Luke Skywalker was struggling to separate from domineering stepparents who pressured him to work on the family farm. Later, he rebelled against imperial domination and fought to overcome the influence of a tyrannical father—Darth Vader. Likewise, George Lucas struggled to separate from a domineering father who pressured him to take over the family business. Later, he rebelled against the Hollywood empire and fought to establish an independent film company far from the reach of Hollywood moguls.

Over the course of the *Star Wars trilogy,* Luke Skywalker gradually evolved from a rebellious teenager with a bad attitude to a Jedi Master who learned to control his darker emotions. The resolution of Luke's internal conflict was paralleled by the resolution of his external conflict with his father—a resolution that led to wholeness both within and without. There was a "character arc" in George Lucas, too. He evolved from an angry renegade to a powerful magnate that transformed the world of filmmaking. The resolution of his inner conflict, i.e., his distrust of authority, was mirrored by his reconciliation with his father and his unparalleled success as a filmmaker.

In both stories, there is a reoccurring pattern of rebellion, transformation, and empowerment on an emotional level. Yet, this pattern is not simply repetition, but shows how Lucas and his alter ego, Luke Skywalker, traversed a path of evolutionary unfoldment. In both stories, each new episode provided an opportunity to learn, develop insight, and realize lunar potentials. Over time there was a progressive development and integration of character.

Just as there was a "key moment" in each film, so there were key moments in the life of George Lucas. His confrontation with death following his car accident, his severance from his father and decision to enter U.S.C. film school, his break with the industry, his determination to establish an independent studio at Skywalker Ranch, and his decision to write *Star Wars,* were all pivotal moments where Lucas had to face a kind of death—rupture with his family, retaliation by Hollywood, financial catastrophe, and so on. One way or the other, the lunar theme of belonging was implicit in these moments; Lucas had to find the courage to trust his feelings and create his *own* family and support system.

If there is a lunar theme in all this, perhaps Lucas sums it up best: "My films have a tendency to promote a personal self-esteem," he says. "Their message is, 'Don't listen to everyone else. Discover your own feelings and follow them. Then you can overcome anything.'"[19] The key phrase here is *discover your own feelings and follow them.* Again, this was the overriding theme of *Star Wars*—trust your feelings—and was the principal moral of the story.*

The Leo-Aquarius sub-theme is also equally present in the life of Lucas and Skywalker. Not only is the *Star Wars* trilogy a testament to the latest advances in film technology, it's about a futuristic society. The film shows an array of computers, druids, robots, bionics, holographs, lasers, and other mechanical gadgets that fairly boggles the imagination. The Moon Aquarius theme is likewise evident in the warmth and caring that exists between the main protagonists of the film. Like family, there is an emotional bond between Han, Luke, Leia, and their two droids, R2D2 and Threepio. As fellow revolutionaries, their love and commitment to the cause binds them.

Likewise, Lucas and his fellow film revolutionaries at Skywalker Ranch constitute a Rebel Alliance of its own sort. From their base in northern California, they've launched powerful technological

---

* Of course, no one part of a chart is entirely responsible for key themes in the native's life. In the end, the whole chart is implicated. Certainly Lucas' first house Sun, which is sextile Mars, gives him a "can do" attitude that is reflected in the action heroes of his films. In this article, however, we are principally interested in how his lunar wound manifests within the context of his career, and how learning to trust his feelings has been a key to his success.

fusillades of special-effects brilliance at their Hollywood rivals, who for nearly a century dominated the film industry.

Luke Skywalker's mission to protect and liberate the fledgling republic from imperial domination is a clear expression of Pluto opposed Moon in Aquarius in the 10th. This role of lunar protector is also present in George Lucas, who's fame and power might obscure the fact that his main mission in life has been to develop films, television shows (*The Young Indiana Jones Chronicles*), and educational materials for the benefit of children. As the prequels make even more clear by telling the story of Darth Vader's youth and eventual fall to the Dark Side, *Star Wars* is both a family saga and a morality play for children.* Long before politicians criticized Hollywood's supposed lack of "family values," Lucas said his "main reason" for making Star Wars "was to give young people an honest, wholesome fantasy life, the kind that my generation had."[20] Today as a divorced father of three children (two of whom he adopted on his own), Lucas asserts, "The most important thing in life is kids."[21]

In addition to opposing Pluto, his Aquarian Moon forms a T-Square to Mercury in the 12th; thus, his caring (Moon) extends to the educational (Mercury) system. Lucas has poured millions of dollars into his subsidiary company, Lucasfilm Learning, to produce innovative software and interactive video games to inject into San Francisco Bay Area classrooms and curricula. Some 18 schools in San Francisco and Marin County served as laboratories for the experimental project. "The way we are educated is based

---

* One could make a case that his Sun square Jupiter in the 4th house is the astrological signature of his focus on "family values." Lucas has a compelling sense of moral obligation to the community. He feels that children today are being corrupted by television because it has no sense of morality (Jupiter). Consequently, he made *Star Wars* as a post-contemporary myth in order that children would again have access to the great mythological traditions and the moral lessons they impart. The point here is that he cares about children. And this is an expression of the Moon.

on 19th century ideals and methods," Lucas said. "Here we are entering the 21st century, and you look at our schools today and say *why are* we doing things this way? Our system of education is locked in a time capsule, and you want to say, 'Hey, you're not using today's tools. Wake up!'"[22]

Again, his Moon Aquarius in the 10th is evident in his dedication to changing the system for the benefit of children. "I'm interested in the future," says Lucas, "and the future is kids."

Space prohibits a more detailed analysis of how the *Star Wars* trilogy is a metaphor for the struggles and triumphs of George Lucas. Suffice to say that an astrological chart depicts a story—a personal myth. And within any good myth there is conflict; conflict is what drives the story forward. Whether it's Luke Skywalker defying the empire, or George Lucas defying Hollywood tradition, the external conflict provides a vehicle for resolving an internal one. Resolution of the inner conflict leads to outer harmony. This was clearly depicted in Lucas' Moon-Pluto opposition. As the tension between these two forces was slowly resolved, each function enriched the other. For Lucas, this meant learning to express powerful feelings of caring concern for the welfare of future humanity—today's children. Toward this end, he has bequeathed us a remarkable gift in the myth of *Star Wars*.

Chapter Four

King Kong and The Venus Complex

A JOURNEY INTO DARKNESS

There is a scene in the recent remake of *King Kong* when Jimmy, who is reading Joseph Conrad's *Heart of Darkness,* asks Mr. Hayes why the hero would go down the river when he *knows* something bad is going to happen. Hayes responds, "He needs to go, to defeat the thing that makes him afraid." This simple statement sums up the primary theme of *King Kong* as well as the core motivations of its central characters. But what *is* the thing that makes them afraid? To answer that, we need to examine the astrological chart of King Kong's writer and producer, Merian C. Cooper.

King Kong is one of the central myths created in the 20th century, a primal dream work that symbolizes a deep and special anxiety of the species. A legendary gorilla in pursuit of a beautiful woman is captured on a primordial island and brought back to civilization where he faces his ultimate fight for survival. The movie's core scenes, imagery, and dialogue has diffused everywhere into the culture. Billed as one of the great love stories of all time, critics unanimously agree that Coopers' 1933 film was an organic work of genius. With King Kong's release, the movie industry was transformed overnight. Its gross of $90,000 over its first weekend was the biggest opening ever. Women were fainting in the isles as the mighty Kong horrified, thrilled, and moved moviegoers of all ages.

King Kong began quite literally as a nightmare. Cooper dreamt one night of a gigantic ape terrorizing New York City and fighting off biplanes from the Empire State Building. He subsequently developed the dream into a screenplay and the rest, as they say, is history. Joseph Campbell pointed out that dreams are personal myths, and myths are public dreams. In Cooper's case, his personal dream *became* a myth precisely because it brilliantly captured a universal human dilemma in symbolic form. Kong's enduring appeal can be understood by analyzing Cooper's birth chart, which contains all of the themes, characters, and elements of the film. In effect, *King Kong* is a symbolization of Merian Cooper's psyche.

COOPER'S BIRTH CHART

Cooper's birth time is not available, so I will focus primarily on his planetary signs and aspects (see chart, next page). Sun conjunct Uranus in Scorpio brands him as a maverick-revolutionary with a penchant for the dark side. Moon Aries adds an adventurous streak to the personality, inciting him to express caring though acts of courage and derring-do.

According to his biography, *Living Dangerously*, Cooper was former WWI flying ace, soldier of fortune, and patriotic war hero who was shot down twice and pronounced dead both times. He went on to become an innovative filmmaker who pioneered Cinerama, and a daring explorer who traveled the far corners of the world, camera in tow, during an era when those corners were still unknown, untamed, and frightening.[1]

The Sun's opening quincunx to Jupiter is also significant, for it suggests that Jupiterian impulses for expansion, travel, and the

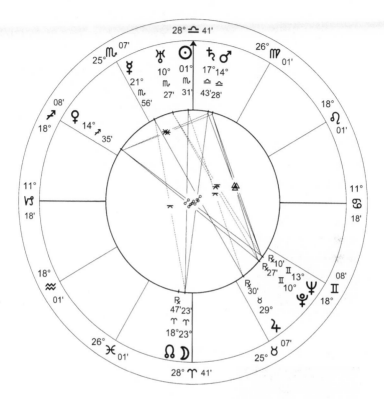

Figure 6: Merian C. Cooper
October 24, 1893, Jacksonville, FL Time Unknown

pursuit of justice were problematic for Cooper. At times he had a tendency to over-reach, to think *too* big. Whether over-extending on a film project, fighting communism with a feral zeal, or plunging headlong into harrowing expeditions in exotic locales, Cooper's Jupiter was a spur and a challenge throughout his life.

These traits are plainly evident in Carl Denham, the character in *King Kong* whom Cooper unabashedly designed as his alter ego. Denham is an intrepid documentary filmmaker and renowned adventurer who sails to a lost island and discovers seemingly prehistoric creatures—all of which Cooper actually did.* Denham is also hotheaded, reckless and financially overextended, and his backers have lost faith in his film project despite his bombastic promise of making a movie so great "they'll have to think up new adjectives when I come back." Likewise, Cooper's actual *King Kong* was one of the great gambles in movie history, and almost didn't get made due to a lack of faith amongst its producers. The comparisons could go on and on. Even Denham's pipe smoking was a noted Cooper affectation, and the stocky, energetic actor who played Denham, Robert Armstrong, bore a distinct physical resemblance to Cooper.**

Another prominent theme in Cooper's chart is his Moon Aries opposition to Saturn in Libra. Whereas the Moon symbolizes our need to belong, its opposition to Saturn suggests this need will be frustrated, requiring Cooper to work extra hard for fulfillment in this area. In 1914, Cooper was expelled for disobedience from the U.S. Naval Academy just months before graduating. Over the next several years he roamed the streets like a penitent suffering for his sins, refusing all help from his family. His go-it-alone code reflected not only his Moon in Aries, but also its opposition to Saturn, which instilled a stoic, disciplined emotional nature and a sense of having to measure up to a high standard in order to feel deserving of love and belonging.

The heroine of *King Kong*, Ann Darrow, certainly embodies this aspect, for we meet her during the great depression in New York where she is struggling as an unemployed actress with no home or family. Saturn has a tendency to depress and deprive, and its opposition to the Moon is aptly symbolized as a sad, lonely,

---

* In 1923 Cooper sailed to the Komodo Islands where he encountered Komodo dragon lizards "as big as canoes," descendents of a prehistoric past.

** Amazingly, they died within 24 hours of one another on April 20-21st, 1973.

destitute woman. Kong, too, embodies the aspect, for he lives a friendless, solitary existence on an unforgiving island, surrounded by enemies (flesh eating dinosaurs) and cut off from civilization.

Denham, Ann, and Kong share a common Aries characteristic: they are all spirited, fierce survivors. With regard to Ann, this is particularly evident in the Peter Jackson remake (2006) in which Ann is depicted as plucky and principled, unwilling to debase herself by working in a strip joint no matter how cold and hungry she might be. Again, we see traces of Cooper's survivor mentality when he wandered the streets after being kicked out of school, determined to go it alone.

THE ARIES-LIBRA DYNAMIC

If Aries signifies all that is primordial, instinctual, and coarse, Libra signifies all that is cultured, civilized, and refined. The Aries-Libra dynamic is especially visible in Cooper's preference for primitive outlands (Moon Aries) and his general disdain for the restraints of civilization (Saturn Libra). Although he made his home in New York and Los Angeles, he was contemptuous of the conceits and conveniences of the modern world. To him, "civilization" was a pejorative for all that was soft and weak.[2] He preferred instead the rough, untamed wilderness—the mountains of Persia, or the jungles of Siam—that provided the locations for his documentaries.

The Aries-Libra conflict is also a central theme of *King Kong,* as evidenced by the Arabian Proverb that Cooper invented for the film's epigraph:

> "And lo, the beast looked upon the face of beauty.
> And it stayed its hand from killing.
> And from that day, it was as one dead."

> —Old Arabian Proverb

Every successful picture had to have a "single strong thought," wrote Cooper, and the key to *Kong* was the beauty-and-the-beast theme,[3] which, of course, is an archetypal expression of the Aries-Libra dialectic. Beauty, kindness, and civility are clearly Libran, whereas our animalistic, bestial and primitive impulses are Aries. References to Beauty and the Beast occur throughout the film, ranging from the opening prologue to the last scene where the policeman and Denham gaze upon the fallen body of Kong. "Well, Denham, the airplanes got him," the policeman mutters. Denham replies, "No, it wasn't the airplanes. Beauty killed the Beast." Earlier in the film, Denham projected that his movie will be a retelling of the ancient legend of Beauty and The Beast. "Beauty softens and attracts and in the end encompasses the destruction of the Beast," says Denham. "He'll lose Ann in the end...and after he does, he'll never be quite the same king of the forest. Brute strength will have yielded to something higher."[4]

That "something higher" was not simply beauty, but *civilization*, which Cooper realized could be symbolized by the highest building in the world—the Empire State Building—that was under construction while he was writing the script. Nature, in contrast, would be personified in the giant gorilla brought low by the guns "of the most modern of weapons, the airplane."[5] In short, civilization (Libra) overcomes the Beast (Aries) made vulnerable by his fatal fascination for Beauty (Libra).

SATURN & MARS OPPOSED MOON

With Saturn and Mars in Libra, Mars (raw aggression) has to be harnessed and controlled by Saturn for the sake of art, beauty, and love (Libra). All of this, however, is at the expense of Moon Aries, which not only opposes Saturn, but also is disposed of by Mars.*

---

* A dispositor is a planet that rules the sign that another planet is in. The disposed planet leads to, and provides a reason for, the actions of its dispositor.

Dispositors signify links in the sequence of action, much as a film will cut from one scene to another. In Cooper's case, every lunar impulse he feels is immediately transferred to Mars, which teams with Saturn to thwart it. Again, this is illustrated in some of the movie's key scenes. When Denham perceives his skipper's protective (lunar) feelings toward Ann, he snaps, "Don't go soft on me Jack." Bound by a responsibility to his art, Denham is not going to let tenderness or sentiments get in the way. As the movie's director (Saturn/Mars), Denham intends is to *use* Ann (Moon) in the service of his artistic vision, regardless of risks to her safety.

This same conflict, but with the roles reversed, is evident in an early scene of *King Kong* when snobby, self-serving business partners (Mars/Saturn) threaten to capsize Denham's bold plans for cinematic adventure by refusing to finance his film (it's too risky). Moreover, Denham's notorious recklessness (Moon Aries) prevents any reputable agent from providing an actress for the expedition. In both instances, Denham feels unsupported and misunderstood. Saturn frustrates the lunar need for support, caring, and understanding.

VENUS AS DISPOSITOR OF SATURN & MARS

Note that Venus disposes both Saturn and Mars, since they tenant the sign that Venus rules (Libra). Like shifting scenes in a movie, Mars/Saturn cuts to Venus in Sagittarius, which is motivated to carry forth the agenda that Mars and Saturn have set into motion. At this point in the film, Denham is flying by the seat of his pants; he has to have an actress *now*. So he steals himself to the challenge and sets out on the streets of New York determined to find a starlet.

It is against this backdrop that Venus makes her entrance. Denham spots the desperate, starving Ann Darrow as she is about to steal an apple from a street side vendor. Stunned by her beauty, he purchases the apple and offers it to her. Then, like the biblical Devil with Eve, he begins to entice and beguile her into contracting with him for the making of his film.

> Denham: Ann I want you to imagine a handsome explorer bound for the Far East. On board ship, he meets a mysterious girl. She's beautiful, fragile, haunted…and she can't escape the feeling that forces beyond her control are compelling her down a road from which she cannot draw back. It's as if her whole life has been a prelude to this moment, this fateful meeting that changes everything. And sure enough, against her better judgment…
>
> Ann: …she falls in love
>
> Denham: *Yes.*
>
> Ann: But she doesn't trust it. She's not even sure if she believes in love.
>
> Denham: Ah, really?
>
> Ann: If she loves someone, it's doomed.
>
> Denham: Why is that?
>
> Ann: Good things never last, Mr. Denham.

Again, all the elements of this scene are strikingly prefigured in the birthchart of Merian Cooper. Venus's sign position (Sagittarius) suggests *what* the individual loves. Sagittarius rules travel and the pursuit of meaning. Ann, the archetype of Venus, is about to go on a sea voyage wherein she will meet and fall in love with a handsome stranger—Carl Driscoll, the playwright she most admires due to his meaningful prose. Sagittarius is also an expansive sign, signifying that which is *big*, which certainly fits her eventual involvement with Kong!

More importantly, however, Venus is opposing a Neptune-Pluto conjunction in Gemini. The dialogue between Denham and

Ann perfectly captures the essence of this combination—a fragile, haunted lover, compelled down a fateful path, falls in love against her better judgment, and is doomed. Denham and Ann's conversation foreshadows what will unfold in the remainder of the story.

VENUS OPPOSED NEPTUNE & PLUTO

Let's consider each aspect separately. Whereas Venus depicts the archetype of beauty and attachment, Pluto signifies sex, transformation, and power. When these two planets are combined in hard aspect, a theme emerges that involves several interrelated dimensions: 1) the association of love with darkness, danger, and death, 2) the fear of, and subsequent repression of, one's desire for intimacy and relatedness; 3) the eroticization of this fear; 4) the re-emergence of repressed desire in the form of an irresistible, overpowering, and dangerous sexual figure; and 5) the potential transformation of fear into love via a willingness to risk death for one's beloved.

All of this may be precipitated by early relational experiences that involve violation, shame, or betrayal, such as occurs in child sexual molestation. More subtle manifestations are certainly possible, but one way or the other the above themes generally emerge out of an early, prototypical event-pattern that involves a wounding (Pluto) in the area of love and attachment (Venus).*

All we know of Ann's past is that her parents are dead and she was bilked out of her inheritance by a corrupt uncle who violated her trust.[6] Certainly, this is in keeping with Venus-Pluto, which rules finances (my money/our money). It sounds as if Ann got "screwed" financially. As for her future, her exchange with Denham pretty

---

* A not uncommon case of a woman with Venus in close opposition to Pluto involved the following. As a child, she was molested repeatedly by her father. She subsequently married a man who physically abused her. Her second marriage was to an FBI officer who died a violent death. Her third was to a man who molested her daughter, and finally she had a long-standing affair with a married man, for which she felt ashamed.

much nailed it. He tells Ann that she will be compelled down a road from which she cannot draw back…a fateful meeting that changes everything. Ann speculates on what the love story is about. Her act of speculation, however, is a projection of her "inner story" about relationship—her fantasy of where love will take her. Ann says she doesn't trust love, and is not even sure she believes in it. If she loves someone, it's doomed because "good things never last."

This outlook typifies someone who has been betrayed, violated, or otherwise wounded by love, and is consistent with Venus in hard aspect to Pluto. We should not be surprised that Ann does not trust love, or that she will be compelled down a fateful path that "changes everything." If healing is to occur, she will need an experience that is so powerful, so deeply moving and transformative, that even the threat of death cannot negate her will to love. Kong will provide her with just that experience.

Venus in opposition to Neptune is no less challenging. Here, the need for love and attachment conflicts with the Neptunian requirement for the development of compassion. As a spiritual impulse, Neptune signifies our need to surrender attachments and become one with the whole. When in hard aspect to Venus, this frequently this takes the form of unrequited love—loving someone who is unavailable because s/he is 1) disinterested; 2) completely unaware of the other's feelings, 3) already in a committed relationship; 4) addicted to a substance from which they must be saved; 5) living in a far-away place; 6) prone to lying, cheating, and promiscuity; or 7) chronically ill or disabled. To this we might add (8) *of another species.*

The point is that loving under any of these circumstances invariably involves sacrifice and loss—sacrifice because one forfeits hope of reciprocal love, and loss because one exists in a more-or-less perpetual state of longing. It is often the case that unconscious guilt (Neptune) underlies this type of self-defeating pattern; the person feels undeserving of relational fulfillment due to some actual or imaginary crime that requires atonement. Very likely this template was laid down in response to childhood events that were either witnessed or experienced.*

Despite its tragic, self-destructive undercurrents, perhaps one is never so close to God as when one loves in this manner, for the Neptunian dimension carries with it a quality of blissful wholeness and unity. Loss, atonement, suffering, all of this brings one closer to the divine in the sense that the need for personal love is sacrificed and in its stead is substituted universal love. By selflessly giving to another with no hope of reciprocity, the individual elevates herself to the status of a saint or divine figure. Paradoxically, this can be intoxicating and addictive even while it may also be masochistic.

A related theme with Venus-Neptune is idealization of the beloved. Figures to whom one is attracted may appear to be numinous beings that transcend the mortal sphere—movie stars, heroes and heroines, gods and goddesses. Of course, this is usually rooted in denial of the other's less than god-like attributes. Disillusionment occurs when they reveal their all-too-human limitations.

Kong's relationship with Ann captures the pathos of the aspect. Ann is unavailable because she is of another species, in love with someone else (Jack Driscoll), and lives in a far-away place. Compounding the problem, Kong is disabled by drugs, stolen from his home, and enslaved. He is, in short, a victim/martyr who inspires pity and terror—Aristotle's prescription for tragedy. The spiritual and chthonic dimensions of Kong are symbolized

---

* A typical case from my files involves a woman who, as a teenager, was caught by her over-involved father with her boyfriend in her bedroom. The father died of a heart attack three days later. Blamed by her family for her father's death, she subsequently atoned for her "crime" by a series of disastrous adult relationships that involved marrying 1) a closet homosexual who deceived her, 2) an alcoholic/pedophile who molested her daughter from her first marriage, and 3) a philanderer who tortured her with endless lies and affairs.

by the Neptune-Pluto conjunction: to the natives he is a god (Neptune), but specifically a god of death and the underworld (Pluto). As the beast-god of Skull Island, Kong symbolizes an ideal of unadulterated masculinity, fearless, instinctive, and all-powerful. Likewise, Ann is an idealized, ultra-feminine creature from a higher (human) dimension that captivates and bewitches. Both are willing to sacrifice themselves for the sake of the other— Kong by his impassioned but disastrous longing for Ann, and Ann by surrendering herself to him at great peril. They both love impossibly, and tragically. All of these elements reflect the Venus-Neptune opposition.

MERIAN COOPER'S VENUS ISSUES

In the case of Marian Cooper, I could find scant biographical evidence that he was prone to any of the more extreme manifestations of Venus-Pluto or Venus-Neptune, which would seem to reflect a relatively integrated, self-actualized character. I believe, for the most part, that Cooper sublimated his Venus configuration into transcendent art that had a magical, mythic quality.* He did, however, father an illegitimate son with one woman and ended up marrying someone else late in life. Despite having vowed eternal bachelorhood, Cooper unexpectedly met the girl of his dreams, actress Dorothy Jordan, during the filming of *King Kong*. He married her that same year (he was 40, she 27). One suspects he married late because he was afraid of commitment. Also, he married secretly, as if love were something to hide, and when he took her on a honeymoon he spent *all* of his money— over a million dollars—not returning to the states until he was completely broke. He then promptly suffered a heart attack.

---

* Among other films, Cooper produced *She* (1935) based on the Rider Haggard novel about an immortal but evil priestess seeking eternal love ("She-Who-Must-Be-Obeyed"). Significantly, Haggard had Venus in the 12th square Neptune in Pisces.

One could argue that Cooper's loss of money and health in the wake of his marriage was self-destructive or at least self-sacrificing. It certainly fits the aspect: love (Venus) is paired with loss (Neptune) and potential death (Pluto). Even if, on the whole, Cooper sublimated his Venus configuration into transcendent art, one might still say, with justification, that his Venus constitutes a psychological complex. Not only is this suggested by his horoscope, it is dramatically illustrated in the imagery and themes of *King Kong*.

King Kong and The Venus Complex

Certain archetypal configurations function like a cramp in the soul, a kind of contraction that signifies a disunity of consciousness. This is Jung's concept of the *complex*—a compact, emotionally charged psychic entity comprised of a group of related, often repressed ideas and impulses that compel distinctive patterns of thought, feeling, and behavior.[7]

A complex can be made up of any natural function (need, drive) that has been repressed—usually due to trauma. Not wanting to remember or re-experience the original event, the drive/need becomes split off and functions autonomously. Like a magnetic vortex in the field of consciousness, the complex draws experiences to itself that eventually enable it to become conscious.

At the center of the complex is an archetype, or cluster of archetypes, which astrologically may be symbolized by hard aspects between inner and outer planets. Venus opposed Neptune/Pluto certainly qualifies, especially given that Neptune and Pluto both symbolize unconscious dimensions of the psyche. By definition, the complex is at least partially unconscious and reveals itself by the emergence of an affect that upsets psychic balance and disturbs customary functioning. Something seems to "take over" that causes the person to respond in uncharacteristic ways—e.g., compelled by forces beyond her control and, against her better judgment, Ann falls in love. Likewise, Kong departs from his usual practice of devouring the native girl and becomes entranced by Ann's beauty, which leads to his capture. Compulsive, self-destructive patterns of behavior typify the complex and have long been associated with Pluto and Neptune.

Once possessed by the complex, the mental and emotional attitude can be rather frightening, and there seems to be little capacity for reason or objectivity. The conscious self is only relatively in control. Behavior turns primitive and extreme since the repressed function has not evolved and, moreover, operates without restraint. Because complexes are made up of functions that appear unintegratable, monsters frequently symbolize them. As Jung put it, "We, from the scientific standpoint, prosaically call the awful beings that dwell in the shadows of the primeval forests, 'psychic complexes'."[8] He elaborates.

> It [the complex] is the *image* of a certain psychic situation that is strongly accentuated emotionally and is, moreover, incompatible with the habitual attitude of consciousness. This image has a powerful inner coherence, it has its own wholeness and, in addition, a relatively high degree of autonomy, so that it is subject to the control of the conscious mind to only a limited extent, and therefore behaves like an animated foreign body in the sphere of consciousness. The complex can usually be suppressed with an effort of will, but not argued out of existence, and at the first suitable opportunity it reappears in all its original strength.[9]

Ann's relationship with Kong illustrates a Venus complex. Kong is discovered on Skull Island, a perfect symbol of the complex in that it depicts a lost, primeval jungle separated from civilization and populated with archaic tribesmen and extinct species. Skull Island symbolizes what we have left behind and repudiated. Surrounded by ominous fog and guarded by an army of dinosaurs, it signifies a break in the unity of consciousness—a splinter psyche with its own wholeness and autonomy. Kong, the monster who resides at the center of the island, emerges into awareness as an emotionally charged, irresistible force with a compulsion to possess the object of his desire (Venus/Ann), a situation clearly incompatible with the intentions of her fellow humans.

All of this metaphorically encapsulates the fear of intimacy depicted astrologically by Venus opposed Neptune/Pluto. While it is the nature of Venus to attract and possess, Neptune/Pluto assures this occurs in relationship to wounding and tragedy. We know Ann doesn't trust love, and for Kong the very impulse must be foreign. His whole existence is one continuous fight for survival, which means his Venus impulse is thrown into shadow, repudiated, and projected outwards. Since he can't afford to love, Ann has to carry his Venus function for him, which is precisely what leads to his sacrifice and ultimate end. Kong cannot control his attraction (Venus), so it overpowers him with tragic consequences. On the other hand, Kong is also the manifestation of *her* Venus in as much as he becomes the dangerous love-object to whom Ann ultimately surrenders.

THE DESCENT AND RETURN OF THE MAIDEN

On Skull Island, themes of death (Pluto) and sacrifice (Neptune) are especially apparent in the scene of Ann as sacrificial object. The natives have abducted her as a bride for Kong, and as such her marriage is equivalent to rape and death. She is placed on a marriage altar, her arms outstretched and bound. The astrological significance of this is profound, for the sacrificial ritual in which Ann is an unwilling participant is the re-enactment of a universal myth that is rooted in seasonal (astrological) phenomena.

Joseph Campbell describes this myth as "the descent and return of the maiden."[10] Perhaps the best-known version is the Greek myth, *Pluto and Persephone*, but this is but one of innumerable stories that developed from observations of the death and rebirth of plant life. Primitive humans observed that at a certain time of the year—autumn—trees lose their leaves, crops wither, and the earth turns gray, which they interpreted as a killing. Six months later, the earth was in full bloom again, seemingly reborn. Moreover, this entire process was reflected by a cosmic procession in which the constellation Scorpio descended with the setting Sun in the fall, thus heralding the death of Nature, and another star-group—Taurus—rose with the Sun in the spring, announcing the return of life. Since Venus is never more than 45 degrees from the Sun, it sets relatively close to the Sun. Sometime around November, as the world dies, Venus descends below the surface of the earth on the western horizon, a phenomenon mythologized as the descent of the maiden into the underworld.

The love-death rituals that developed in response to these events were re-enactments of *The Descent And Return Of The Maiden*. Since this myth personifies seasonal processes as gods and links them to corollary celestial objects, the love-death ritual imitated the seasonal-celestial drama. A maiden is killed and figuratively descends into the underworld to mate with its presiding god. Since she embodies the will of the people, they all have union with the god through her. The ritual not only declares the community is in sync with the gods, thus assuring social harmony and economic wellbeing; it is also a way of *identifying* with the gods and thereby claiming some of their power.

Campbell describes a rite among the cannibal gardeners of New Guinea, approximately where Skull Island is fictionally located, that is shockingly similar to the sacrificial rite in *King Kong*. A virginal maiden (Venus) is offered as a sacrifice to a god of death

(Pluto), and then, amidst much dancing and drumming, she is killed and eaten. The ritual is a re-enactment of what happens in the fall when the god of the underworld kills life and eats it, which was thought to be a necessary precursor to life's resurrection in the spring. Through such a ritual, the tribe celebrates and embodies the required attitude toward Nature for that phase of the year: a willingness to die in order that life can be renewed.

In effect, *King Kong* is a variation on the myth of the descent and return of the maiden, complete with the corresponding love-death ritual sacrifice. A god of death abducts a virginal maiden into the underworld where she becomes his queen, a fate synonymous with rape and death. The beast-god takes the maiden to his cave deep in the heart of Skull Island, where he proceeds to undress her, a figurative rape.* Through her relationship with the god, the maiden is transformed. Eventually she "returns" to civilization, renewed and empowered by the experience.

It is important to recognize that the myth of *The Descent And Return Of The Maiden* metaphorically encapsulates the seasonal processes occurring during the Taurus-Scorpio phases of the year. The myth is, in effect, an expression of the Taurus-Scorpio axis. That Cooper was attracted to this myth, as evidenced by his making of *King Kong*, must reflect his identification with it. This should not be surprising since his Taurus-Scorpio polarity is highlighted by virtue of the opposition between its planetary representatives, Venus and Pluto. Moreover, Pluto disposes his Sun, thus establishing that Cooper's identity is closely linked to the god of the underworld. He once exclaimed in an interview, "I *am* King Kong."[11] Since self-expression (Sun) triggers the

---

* This was most clearly established in the original 1933 *King Kong* when Kong peels off the clothes of an unconscious Ann, sniffs his fingers, and so on. While some authors have argued that this scene reflects either a rape fantasy or an act of child sexual molestation, it would be shortsighted to think that this is the ultimate meaning of the film.

Pluto-Neptune conjunction and its opposition to Venus, it would appear that Cooper is at odds with his will to love. Death and loss are polarized to Venus; yet, inextricably entwined with it. Recall that Cooper spent all of his money and suffered a near-fatal heart attack the same year that he married.

It is significant that in Cooper's version of the myth, Kong is unwilling to release Ann from the underworld; instead, she is rescued by Carl Driscoll, with Kong in close pursuit. I suspect this reflects Cooper's personal struggle with his Venus complex, which, if unintegrated, can manifest in two distinct ways vis-à-vis relationship: 1) jealously and hopeless entanglement, or 2) complete avoidance. Both behavioral strategies are designed to ward off the vulnerability to pain, loss and suffering that is a likely consequence of the aspect. Initially, both Kong and Ann avoid intimacy, but this soon reverses into its counterpart—jealousy and hopeless entanglement.

ANIMA AND ANIMUS

According to Jung, the particular circumstances surrounding our relationship with the opposite sex are determined by the relative degree of integration we have achieved within ourselves. Each individual, male and female, carries within a specific unconscious image that personifies the nature of his or her other half. Called the *anima* and *animus*, the anima is the female personification of the man's unconscious, while the animus is the male personification of the woman's unconscious.

The secret aim of the unconscious, said Jung, was to bring about relationships that provide opportunities to develop and integrate disowned parts of the self. It follows that the anima/animus image is potentially a guide to the depths of the unconscious. There are countless examples from film and literature that depict the anima as an alluring, mysterious figure tempting man to follow her up the dangerous path that leads to his liberation and salvation. As a guide and facilitator of the transformation process, she is a connecting link that accompanies his transition from one state of reality to another.

Essentially dream images, anima and animus are first experienced in projected form, thereby determining who is attractive and expectations of what is likely to happen. It is necessary to meet the anima/animus in projected form; otherwise, these images remain locked in the unconscious and are not released to create the struggles that bring with them the potential for a deepening and widening of consciousness.

Specific characteristics of the anima/animus serve as compensations for masculine and feminine conscious attitudes. Antagonism and fear in close personal relationships is likely to indicate being out of touch the anima/animus. When the conscious attitude is carried to a negative extreme, it will tend to produce a corresponding negative attitude toward the opposite sex, e.g., the "macho male" is likely to image an anima figure as clinging and dependent. This inner split will be reflected in eventual conflict and confusion with actual lovers to the extent that each person remains unbalanced.

There is no single factor in the horoscope that represents the anima or animus, for such an image is a conglomerate of multiple parts. It would be fair to presume, however, that Venus' sign, house, and aspects will be relevant, since Venus rules relationships. To see how this works, consider that Kong is a stand-in for Marian Cooper. As Kong's anima symbol, Venus in Sagittarius suggests that Kong will be attracted to a woman from another culture who will expand his horizons. Further, Pluto's opposition to Venus suggests this anima figure could lead to transformation, but at great personal risk. Neptune opposed Venus also hints at an idealized anima that could result in disillusionment, loss, and grief, which are necessary for the development of empathy and compassion.

Clearly, Ann Darrow meets all of Kong's anima criteria.

At its most unintegrated state, Venus opposed Neptune suggests a relationship that, to borrow Ann's words, is "doomed because good things never last." Compounding the problem, Pluto in hard aspect to Venus often goes to extremes in order to avoid dreaded outcomes associated with intimacy. For example, to avoid the pain of rejection or betrayal, the person may become pathologically controlling, coercive, or intimidating (stalking, intense jealousy, spousal abuse), all of which describes Kong's initial behavior toward Ann.

Since the relationship between conscious and unconscious is compensatory, the greater the disparity, the more extreme the anima/animus becomes as a counterpart to the one-sided conscious attitude. Kong is masculinity carried to its most frightening extreme; thus, his anima (*Ann*-ima), drifting out the oceanic unconscious, is pure unadulterated femininity. He is huge and all-powerful, a king of the jungle; Ann is comparatively small and weak, a starving actress in New York reduced to an abject state on Skull Island. The tension generated between these two poles—omnipotent god and impotent victim—comprises the first half of the film. To resolve the tension, each party must be willing to surmount fear and integrate their opposite, even if this means loss or death.

ENANTIODROMIA

On Skull Island, a transformation begins to take place. Following her initial abduction, Ann decides to stand-up to Kong, holding her ground in the face of his terrifying, intimidating fury. She subsequently entertains him, and even defies him by refusing to play his game of knock-the-damsel-down. After the battle with the T-Rexes in which Kong risks his life to save Ann, trust is fully established. Now Ann *wants* to be with him. At the cliff edge out-side Kong's cave, they gaze at the setting Sun. Ann signs to Kong, "beautiful," and the beast-god gently extends his hand, inviting her to rest in the softness of his palm. She settles down for the night—queen of the underworld.

Jack Driscoll's subsequent rescue of Ann has multiple levels of meaning. As an act of saving, it is an example of Venus-Neptune: Driscoll is willing to sacrifice his life for Ann. In Ann's case, however, it is more complicated. She wants to be rescued, of course, but abandoning Kong for Driscoll is an act of double betrayal, for not only has she broken a fragile trust that had just been established, but unwittingly she has become a pawn in Denham's plans to capture Kong and exploit him for personal gain. When she realizes this, her guilt is palpable, and her compassion for Kong intensifies. Abandonment, betrayal, subsequent guilt and need for atonement—these are classic themes of Venus in opposition to Neptune and Pluto.

By the time they arrive in New York, there has been a complete reversal of roles. Whereas Ann was the sacrificial victim on the altar waiting for Kong, now Kong is the enslaved captive waiting on a stage for Ann. His chained, outstretched arms denote his complete and total subjugation, a mirror of Ann's position on Skull Island. Jung referred to this as *enantiodromia*—the tendency for things to revert to their opposite. If one side of a pair of opposites becomes excessively predominant in the personality, it is likely to turn into its contrary. This is because the psyche has an innate tropism toward balance, or wholeness.

The evolution of Ann and Kong's relationship depicts the gradual integration, or balancing, of Venus *with* Neptune and Pluto. In fact, this is what an opposition requires: balance, harmony, and collaboration between the respective planets such that each is enriched by its relationship with the other. For this to occur, however, there must be a willingness to fully experience whatever the aspect brings.

Recall that the complex draws experiences to itself that allow it to gain entrance into consciousness. It was Kong's legend that drew Denham and the crew of the *Venture* to Skull Island, which provided the catalyst for his transformation from a one-sided, hyper-male monster to a vulnerable creature willing to die for love. Likewise, Ann's disempowered state as a starving actress ultimately led her to Kong, wherein she overcomes her fear of intimacy as evidenced by her intent to find Kong during his rampage in New York. She is willing to jeopardize her safety, and even sacrifice herself, for the chance to be with him one last time—all this for a creature that initially embodied a fate worse than death.

Like the complex, Kong can be temporarily suppressed—drugged and chained—but at first suitable opportunity he reasserts himself in all his original strength. Breaking free from the chains that bind him, Kong's intense desire for Ann illustrates the fatal fascination connected to the eroticized anima/animus, the irresistible urge to be united with one's other half, regardless of the consequences.

When Ann finally comes, she gives herself to him with such tenderness that the audience cannot help but be moved. Her soothing presence transforms his rage from murderous intent to a playful frolic on the ice ponds of Central Park. It is a sublime reunion with the lost love-object. As Kong finds his balance on the ice, they slide and flow and spin in joyous ecstasy; an idyllic, enchanting scene of luminous beauty, full of grace and power—apt testimony to the integration of Venus with Neptune and Pluto. As Jung put it, "the reintegration of a personal complex has the effect of release and often of healing."[12]

CLIMAX

In the final segment, Ann and Kong literally transcend the world below as they ascend to the top of the Empire State Building. The scene encapsulates the ethereality of Venus-Neptune love—its heights and aspirations, its fragility, and finally its hopelessness, crushing disillusionment, and fall. For the moment, however, like gods upon the pinnacle of Mount Olympus, they have escaped the restraints and limitations of the world below.

Looking out at the rising Sun, Kong touches his heart and gazes at Ann. She realizes he is communicating with her in a conscious, deliberate way for the first time, mimicking her gesture for the word "beautiful" that she unwittingly taught him on Skull Island. "Yes, beautiful," Ann responds with wondrous awe. It is a final tribute to Venus, an otherworldly moment of exquisite beauty and infinite love. Yet, just as Ann predicted, their love is doomed. Loving a god (or god-substitute) on a personal level can never last, for Venus opposed Neptune decrees that such a love is but a vehicle for the development of a greater kind of love—compassion for victims, empathy for suffering, and selfless devotion to a spiritual ideal. A capacity for that type of love can only develop through experiences of loss and bereavement.

Yet, even as the bullets are ripping into Kong's chest and the life slowly drains from his eyes, there is triumph. Ann attempts to save him by positioning herself between the wounded Kong and the airplanes that seek to kill him, but her efforts are futile. Kong rescues her again as she falls from the ladder, but he cannot save himself. Kong and Ann have yielded to something higher; beast has become beauty, and beauty beast, and love has conquered fear. It is in their willingness to die, to suffer for love's sake, to sacrifice for the other and be transformed into something greater, that the full integration of Venus opposed Neptune/Pluto is realized.

DENOUEMENT

In the end of course, it is still a tragedy, and the viewer may rightly ask: *why did they do it? Why did they love so impossibly?* Of course, to answer this question in any realistic way, one has to view the film as a metaphor of a common human predicament. If love (Venus), is thrown into shadow as a consequence of early experiences that make the very impulse seem risky, dangerous, or even self-destructive, then one is likely to attract a relationship that is consonant with one's internal, albeit unconscious convictions; that is, one falls in love, but in a context that conforms to one's story *about* love. By living out the internal story, two things become possible: 1) the story becomes objectified and thus conscious, and 2) one then has the opportunity to refute the self-defeating, disempowering ideas that generate the troubling predicament.

So why did they do it, why did they love so impossibly? The long answer would be some version of what's written above. However, if Marian C. Cooper were around, I suspect he would simply say: "To defeat the thing that makes them afraid."

Chapter Five

The Saturn-Pluto Opposition of 2001-2002

TURNING TERROR INTO TRIUMPH

Sheldon Kopp, in his picture book, *What Took You So Long,* shows a butcher holding a chicken he is about to kill. The caption says, "Sometimes things are as bad as they seem." After the attack on the New York World Trade Center, I imagine that at least some of us felt like that chicken—things had suddenly gone bad. There was a grave threat, a dark menace loose in the world, and despite your best efforts to carry on as if nothing had changed, deep in your gut you felt something new and persistent and unwanted.*

By now all of us are familiar with how 9/11 encapsulated the most horrific dimension of the Saturn-Pluto opposition. Rather than simply regurgitate this and other surface manifestations of the aspect, I want to go a little deeper and see if we can get at its underlying dynamics and purpose. In so doing, we will reflect on how Saturn-Pluto has operated over 2001-2002 to actually

---

* S. Kopp metaphor borrowed from a Mark Skousen newsletter long since lost.

make the world a *better* place.* This may seem strange given the horrendous events we witnessed throughout 2001-2002. However, there is actually an abundance of evidence to suggest that the world has been going through birth pangs in the process of transforming itself into a new, more complex order.

Just to set the stage, let's briefly review some dates. A full Saturn-Pluto cycle takes approximately 32-37 years. The previous opposition was in 1965 and the next one won't be until 2035. The opposition in '65 kicked off the revolutionary sixties and here we are now in what Jean Houston calls "the spirit quaking times". Within this most recent opposition, Saturn and Pluto were exact on August 5th, 2001, again on November 2nd during its retrograde phase, and a third and final time on May 25th of the following year, 2002.

In thinking about the Saturn-Pluto opposition, it's easy to assume that its effects are limited to the political arena where they have been most obvious. Certainly the global war on terrorism is the most blatant manifestation of the aspect, along with the continuing threat of nuclear proliferation and biological warfare— subjects that seem constantly to be in the news over this period. In fact, however, Saturn-Pluto dynamics were evident in many facets of reality. We saw it in the world of business with the Enron Scandal and the economic recession, in science with the controversy over stem cell research and human cloning, and in the crisis of the Catholic Church brought on by pedophile priests and the rape of a nation.

Rick Levine tracked this aspect all the way back to the pre-Christian era, and always it seems to correspond to the same

---

* This chapter was written in 2002-2003 when many of these events were fresh in the news. While some of the references seem dated now, the main point of this chapter is independent of any particular dates or events – namely, that world transits are purposive. It is important to glean not only *how* Saturn opposed Pluto correlated to the major themes and occurrences of 2001-2002, but more importantly, *why*. Discerning the purpose of a transit is more meaningful than simply listing what did or might happen.

momentous events—wars and revolts, the rise and fall of nations, revolutions—including scientific ones, such as the beginning of the nuclear age in 1947 with the harnessing of nuclear power.* Significantly, it also corresponds to the history of war between the West and the Middle East. Here's one example of many.

On November 27, 1095, when Saturn and Pluto were quincunx, Pope Urban gave one of history's most famous speeches to the Council of Clermont in France, calling for a holy war against Islam to unite factious Europe.** Dr. E.L. Skip Knox of Boise State University in Idaho summarized the Pope's speech:

> The noble race of Franks must come to the aid of their fellow Christians in the East. The infidel Turks are advancing into the heart of Eastern Christendom; Christians are being oppressed and attacked; churches and holy places are being defiled. Jerusalem is groaning under the Saracen yoke. The Holy Sepulchre is in Moslem hands and has been turned into a mosque. ...The Franks [Germans] must stop their internal wars and squabbles. Let them go instead against the infidel and fight a righteous war. God himself will lead them, for they will be doing His work. There will be absolution and remission of sins for all who die in the service of Christ. Here they are poor and miserable sinners; there they will be rich and happy. Let none hesitate; they must march next summer. God wills it!

And so Pope Urban set into motion two centuries of bloody battle. Two different medieval cultures, the 11th-century Catholic and the 11th-century Muslim, had locked in a death struggle in their mutual attempts to drive each other out of the holy land.

With their battle cry of "Deus vult!" (God wills it), the Catholics were often victorious against the Muslims. In the summer of 1099,

---

* See "Saturn-Pluto Cycles" by R. Levine at http://www.stariq.com/Main/Articles/P0003039.htm
** The following account of the crusades is from Thom Hartmann's article, "The Goddess of Democracy," which is from *From the Ashes: A Spiritual Response to The Attack on America.*

when Saturn and Pluto were exactly opposed (as they were in 2001-2002), Medieval historian Raymond of Agiles wrote the following eyewitness account of the attack and seizure of Jerusalem by the triumphant Crusaders.

> "Some of our men cut off the heads of their enemies; others shot them with arrows, so that they fell from the towers; others tortured them longer by casting them into the flames. Piles of heads, hands, and feet were to be seen in the streets of the city. It was necessary to pick one's way over the bodies of men and horses. But these were small matters compared to what happened at the temple of Solomon, a place where religious services were ordinarily chanted. What happened there? If I tell the truth, it will exceed your powers of belief. So let it suffice to say this much at least, that in the temple and portico of Solomon, men rode in blood up to their knees and bridle reins."

Not surprisingly, given the horrific nature of the previous report, Richard Tarnas describes Saturn-Pluto as "the heaviest, the darkest, most weighty, mortally serious, [and] historically grave of all archetypal combinations."* He also notes that the aspect is capable of bringing about enduring social-political transformations. While there are unquestionably some grim, darkly despairing themes associated with Saturn-Pluto dynamics, I agree with Richard that there is also something hopeful.

A few years ago I attended a lecture by Rob Hand at the NCGR conference in Hartford, and I was struck by something he said. At the end of his talk, he referred to his TMA article on Saturn-Pluto, which he'd written earlier that summer before the September 11th attack.** He said that he was actually disturbed by his own article, as

---

* See "An Astrological Perspective on the World Trade Center Attack" by R. Tarnas at http://www.stariq.com/Main/Articles/P0003039.htm.

** See "A Crisis of Power: Saturn and Pluto face off," by R. Hand, Aug/Sep 2001, *The Mountain Astrologer.*

despite it's accuracy in more or less predicting the conflict between the US and the middle east, his predictions were not *useful*—at least not in the sense of being able to do anything about the events in question. He then suggested that perhaps mundane, predictive astrology should not be merely descriptive, but also *prescriptive* in the same sense that modern, psychological astrology tries to be.

What I want to suggest is that Saturn-Pluto dynamics actually may constitute a prescription of their own. There are certain healing, transformative effects implicit in Saturn-Pluto that underlay its more obvious destructive manifestations. In other words, the aspect is its *own* prescription, and it works itself out *through* humankind whether we realize it or not. Of course, the value of astrology is that it allows us to step outside this process and see it objectively, which, in turn, enables us to work *with* it in a conscious, intentional way.

Jung said that neurosis is suffering yet to find its meaning. A human being could endure just about anything, thought Jung, as long as his suffering had meaning. So when something painful occurred to one his patients, Jung would ask, "What did the event happen *for?*" In other words, what was the event's purpose and significance? What was it requiring *from* the individual? If we apply this approach to understanding collective trends and events, we might ask, "What is the purpose of the recent Saturn-Pluto opposition for collective humanity?" Obviously, its purpose is not simply to inflict mortal terror and suffering on a global scale. Rather, we might wonder how these events are furthering a divine intent, a cosmic plan.

Astrology can be enormously helpful in this regard, not simply as a predictive tool for telling us what could or might happen, but rather to ask in retrospect, "What are the events that are happening happening *for?*"

SATURN

I think of planets as processes; that is, planets are active and dynamic. Each planet symbolizes a set of interrelated actions conducive toward a goal. Saturn, for example, represents the action of structuring, organizing, and planning. We might say its goal is the achievement of perfection—perfect order and control, which is a feeling of *success* relative to the affairs ruled by its sign position and the planets it aspects.

Saturnian processes manifest through various roles and phenomena. Father figures, bosses, authorities, organizations, governments, rules, and regulations all relate to Saturn functions of controlling, regulating, managing, planning, administering, and the like. The important thing to keep in mind is that Saturn is a series of actions conducive toward a goal, actually a *long-term* goal, which I'm saying is the goal of perfect form, order, and control. Of course, we never attain perfection, at least not on a regular or permanent basis. Like all archetypal principles, Saturn is a work in process. When something or someone doesn't measure up the standard, Saturn demands *accountability,* a key Saturn word.

PLUTO

Like Saturn, Pluto is a process, too. It symbolizes a set of interrelated actions—transforming, healing, and regenerating. These are the usual words we hear associated with Pluto. In astrology, however, we use words like healing and transformation like we're talking about breakfast cereals. What does it really mean to "transform" something? The prefix *trans* of transform means "over, beyond." And form, of course, means structure. So to *trans*form something means to move it beyond its current form into a new, more evolved structure. Usually, this means a structure that is more complex and integrated. Otherwise, the old form would prevail and evolution would not occur. So, transformation essentially means to change the nature, function, or condition of something from a simpler to a more complex state. Close cousins are words like *reform, convert, overhaul, rebuild,* and *reorganize.*

These processes don't occur without a certain amount of pain and suffering, mostly because transformation requires that something be *eliminated.* We often miss this about Pluto: its association with processes of elimination. On an organic level, Pluto rules the eliminative organs of the body along with their terminal end points, the anus and urethra. To purge, cleanse, and eliminate that which is indigestible and thus toxic or destructive to a system is Plutonian.*

Plutonian processes not only have to do with elimination, but also with *integration,* i.e., Pluto symbolizes a process of assimilating what is outside a system *into* the system, thereby regenerating the old order. Integration, in turn, requires allowing a substance, or an entity, to *penetrate* the boundary that separates what is inside from what is outside the system. Thus, Pluto rules actions that have to do with *penetrating,* probing, and piercing—or, looked at from the inside, of ingesting, taking in, of being penetrated. Of course, if penetration is unwanted or forced, it constitutes a violation, or rape, something for which the mythological Pluto is infamous.

Once a system is penetrated, what is useful can then be incorporated, metabolized, and assimilated; what is not useful is excreted. Again, this is what integration means: to convert an outside agent into the system's existing internal structure, eliminating that which is unassimilatable, and thereby regenerating the system. The cells of our bodies are constantly regenerating themselves in just this way.

---

* When I use the word "system," I am referring to any assemblage of parts with relations between them. This can be an individual, a company, a government, a nation, or a community of nations. An astrological chart is itself a system made up of parts (planets) with relations (aspects) between them. Thus astrology is perfect for symbolizing the organization of systems on various levels.

On a socioeconomic level, processes of regeneration are brought about by financial transactions; we convert funds—taxes, investments—into whatever is necessary to maintain the organization of a system, be it a business or government. Pluto, therefore, rules all manner of monetary flows, or economics in general.

If Pluto has a goal, I would say it's the restoration of integrity, or wholeness, which gives a feeling of power. Power is a function of integrity. To the extent that a system is not integrated, i.e., in conflict with itself or with another system, it lacks power—or, put another way, to the extent that something inside or outside a system threatens its existence, the system loses power. By eliminating that which is destructive to the system, power and wholeness is restored. On a sociopolitical level, what needs to be eliminated is crime, terrorism, corruption—in a word, evil—which can be defined as any action that causes harm, pain, or injury to a social system.

Transformation can be broken down into three phases:

1. To **penetrate** (or **be penetrated**).

2. To **assimilate** what can be used for purposes of regeneration.

3. To **eliminate** what is toxic or destructive.

DEATH AND REBIRTH

Pluto is also associated with death and rebirth. Occasionally something threatens a system that is so toxic and destructive that the system cannot assimilate it without dying to its old order and rebuilding an entirely new one that incorporates the threatening agent. But this is scary because it constitutes a kind of death. So the system may initially attempt to create an impenetrable barrier against the feared thing. Thus a shadow is created, something the system regards as inferior, destructive, or evil.

If it's a biological system, think of a lethal virus or toxic agent that causes cancer. If it's a political system, think terrorists, which are analogous to cancer "cells." We even describe terrorists in terms of a network of decentralized "terrorist cells" that communicate with one another and have a common purpose: to penetrate a targeted system and destroy it. This is what a suicide bomber does, whether it's a Boeing 767 crashing into the World Trade Center, or a 19-year old Palestinian girl that walks into an Israeli cafe and blows herself up. Again, that which is *evil* is whatever is destructive to the integrity of the system.

Eventually, if real transformation is to occur, the system must integrate the feared thing, must try to assimilate it, for otherwise healing and evolution is prevented and the system stagnates. Transformation is different than mere regeneration. When a system regenerates, it doesn't actually change its internal structure. Regeneration is rebirth, but without death. The cells in our body are constantly undergoing a process of self-regeneration. Whereas transformation and regeneration both require the purging of destructive, toxic elements, transformation goes one step further: it involves integrating something that will fundamentally and irrevocably *change* the system's internal structure. To transform entails a process of death *and* rebirth.

CRISES AND EVOLUTION

In psychological terms, the thing that must be assimilated is *the shadow,* which initially is ejected or projected out of the system into the environment. It seems to be a general principle of evolution that the rejected element eventually induces a crisis in the environment, which, at a certain point, no longer supports the system's current structure. The shadow is precisely what the system cannot assimilate, i.e., its "waste," which once dissipated into the surrounding medium creates those conditions that ultimately destabilize the system. It's an evolutionary feedback process: projection changes the environment, which, in turn, impacts upon the system and throws it into crisis. The system responds to this self-induced perturbation by reorganizing at a higher level that *integrates* the formerly rejected "waste product" responsible for the crisis.

Crises are as natural to Pluto as order is to Saturn. It is interesting to note that the Chinese character for crisis is actually a combination of two characters, one of which means "danger," and the other, "opportunity." This is essentially what's been happening to all things Saturnian in the world. They are undergoing a crisis, which is dangerous to be sure, but also an opportunity for transformation.

Throughout 2001-2002, there was an extraordinary proliferation of revolutions and revolts that impinged upon governments all over the world—against the United States, Israel, Pakistan, Yemen, Russia, India, Indonesia, the Philippines, Angola, the Congo, Columbia, Brazil, Argentina, and on and on. Revolution is ideally in the service of reform. Ultimately, if true transformation is to occur, there must be an *integration* of the threatening agent into the system, thereby bringing about its death and rebirth into a new, higher order. We see this in the rebuilding of Afghanistan, which is integrating western democratic principles into its political system. Afghanistan's transformation encapsulates what is happening globally on a more subtle level—a virtual rebuilding and reorganization of the world-order.

THE OPPOSITION

Crises clearly are dangerous times. From Saturn's perspective, these processes of transformation have to be controlled, managed, and restrained in order that they don't become merely destructive. If Pluto is crisis, and Saturn is management, then "crisis management" is one obvious meaning of Saturn-Pluto. We can also think of Saturn as pressure, and Pluto is upheaval; thus Saturn-Pluto is like a pressure cooker with the heat turned up dangerously high. The opposition is when the lid blows off. Let's think about this for a moment.

First, the opposition is an aspect of relationship. The goal of an opposition is to unite warring opposites and create a partnership between two planetary functions. Because the two planets oppose one another, the opposition is an aspect of **objective awareness**. It has a quality of bringing something into view; it's in your face, each planet has to engage the other, whether in love or war. The opposition is like bringing a picture into focus on a camera; what was fuzzy background suddenly comes into sharp focus; it comes into view. Saturn actually enhances this quality, because Saturn has to do with facing reality, as in "face the facts, face the music." In this case, Saturn (government, authority, the rule maker) has to face Pluto—that which is potentially transformative or destructive to the existing order.

The best example here is terrorism—Pluto. It's not like Bin Laden and Al Qaeda sprung full born out of the cosmos on September 11th. They had been operating since 1989. Likewise, the Taliban ruled Afghanistan for seven years before we suddenly noticed there was a problem on September 11th. Since then we've become more *fully aware* (think *full* Moon) of a number of things: the malignant militancy of Islamic fundamentalism, the tragic plight of Afghan women under Taliban rule, the suicidal rage and despair of Palestinian youth, the numbing poverty and hopelessness in 3rd world countries that provides a breeding ground for terrorism, the connection between drugs and terrorism, and a host of other evils. We have also become more aware of Plutonic elements within our own country. Corruption and greed within the American corporate culture (e.g., Enron) and pedophilia within the Catholic Church being two of the more obvious examples, though these things, too, have been with us for a long time.

Ideally with an opposition, the planets *complete* **themselves through one another.** By "completion" I mean attain a state of balance. The planetary functions have to *engage* one other, explore how they can link up and collaborate, and adjust their natures to accommodate one another. When working optimally, the respective functions will cooperate in a mutually beneficial fashion. Each function will compromise somewhat in order to coordinate with the opposing function; each will balance and check the other's extremism.

I think the best example of this was the new political alliances that formed over 2002 as a consequence of the war on terror. Whereas at the last conjunction of 1982, the cold war was at its peak, at the opposition of 2002 United States and Russia became allies. In May, for the first time in history, NATO—the North Atlantic Treaty Organization—approved a partnership with Russia for cooperation on terrorism, arms control, and crisis management. British Foreign Secretary Jack Straw said, "This is...the funeral of the Cold War. It's marks a profound historical change. With This, Russia comes out of the cold as a partner, ally and friend of NATO." In addition to Russia, there were unprecedented negotiations with China, Pakistan, Iran, Saudi Arabia, and other Middle Eastern countries in an effort to collaborate in countering the terrorist threat.

U.S. Intelligence agencies also began cooperating with each other and with government officials in a manner that was unprecedented. The FBI, CIA, and INS (Immigration and Naturalization Service) are analogous to components of the immune system of the body politic. Designed to counter threats to national security, they perform a Pluto function of assimilation and elimination. These agencies have traditionally operated independent from one another. Since 9/11, however, significant changes have been made in the way threat information is studied and circulated within the government.

For the first time, the CIA and FBI began comparing notes on all terrorist threat information that came in each day. Their daily "threat report" is then distributed to senior policy makers within the government—Saturn—including the then White House director of homeland security, Tom Ridge. It provided a structure for discussion among senior officials as to how to evaluate threats and determine appropriate strategies. In effect, the Saturn-Pluto structure for intelligence gathering—our immune system—became more integrated, complex, and efficient in combating threats to national security. And this was a direct consequence of a new level of cooperation (opposition) between the government (Saturn) and the intelligence community (Pluto).

When not working optimally, however, the opposition is an aspect of conflict. There can be vacillation between the two functions with a tendency to feel caught between two sides of an issue. For example, there had been controversy within America as to whether we should entirely blame Islamic fundamentalists for 9/11, or whether we should shoulder some responsibility for the conditions that led to the terror. Was America simply the victim of an unjustified attack? Or was the greed, insensitivity, spiritual bankruptcy, exploitation, and profit-at-any-price imperialist mentality that characterizes our transnational corporations responsible? While bombing the World Trade Center can hardly be justified, some feel that our foreign policy of supporting corrupt Middle Eastern governments in order to protect our oil interests has unwittingly contributed to a political climate that foments terror. Obviously, the issue can be argued from both sides.

The inability to integrate both sides results in a seesaw quality. One planet is expressed at the expense of the other, up and down, back and forth, but never meeting in the middle. The expression of one planet at a time tends to create a pattern of symmetrical escalation as each planet vies for dominance. Saturn tries to prevent Plutonic excesses—violence, destruction—by instituting rigid controls, and Pluto revolts against Saturnian oppression through acts of terror and subversion.

In the political situation of 2001-2002, one can make a case for both sides being excessive. Many people felt that the distribution of wealth and power within the world was obscenely out of balance—a relatively small percentage of people control the majority of the world's financial resources while three billion people earn less than $2 a day. On the other hand, the extremes to which insurrectionists are willing to go to redress the imbalance—sending Anthrax laced letters to U.S. Congressman, utilizing heroin profits to buy arms, forcing children into the military in Uganda—is far worse than the evil they seek to supplant; if, indeed, it even is evil.

Another example of lack of balance was the Israeli-Palestinian conflict. Israel plays Saturn, the dominant other, and tries to control Palestinians and bring about order. Yet, the more they oppress their neighbors, the more Plutonic rage they evoke—to the point that Palestinian children are willing to blow themselves up just to have an impact on their oppressors. Yet, the more Palestinians revolt, the more Israel feels compelled to suppress them. It's an escalating cycle of violence with neither side having a positive influence. Of course, this cycle of violence seems endless and can hardly be correlated to a specific transit. During 2001-2012, however, the Israeli-Palestinian conflict seemed to intensify as part of the larger war on terror.

Oppositions are also aspects of projection. Processes of identification and projection cause the oscillating, back-and-forth quality of the opposition. Whichever planet is identified with, the other gets projected. It's interesting that the Taliban sees the west as the evil Satan (Pluto), whereas they were the restorers of order (Saturn) within war-torn Afghanistan after the withdrawal of Soviet forces. We, of course, see *them* as the forces of darkness.

Each side projects Pluto onto the other. Ideally, externalization of conflict in oppositions leads to increased awareness of both planetary functions, and the relationship becomes the vehicle through which the two functions gradually become integrated. The opposition is ultimately an aspect of dialogue, reconciliation, and mediation.

It's as if Saturn looks at Pluto and says, "Tell me, Pluto, what do I have to do to heal myself, to become totally organized, intensely efficient, ruthlessly economical, and passionately devoted to bringing about a beneficent world order wherein no one is oppressed but everyone is respectful of the law." And Pluto says, "Why yes, I'd be glad to tell you, but please, would you help *me* do my job better, too? Help me bring myself under control so that I can reform systems without needlessly harming them, become better disciplined at eliminating evil, more effective in regenerating the degenerate, systematic in healing the sick, and methodical in purging corruption. Help me to bring about a truly global integration among nations, a transformed world culture, with a more equitable distribution of power, wealth, and prosperity. Can you help me with that, Saturn?"

MUTUAL PLANETARY INFLUENCE

If each planet has its own purpose, then they have a **joint purpose** when in aspect. Not only must they cooperate, but also each takes into itself a bit of the other's essence. An aspect is like a planetary transfusion process or cosmic alchemy in which some kind of amalgamation is created which yields emergent properties that neither planet possesses by itself.

Saturn, for example, is going to *Saturnize* all things Plutonian. It's going to try and manage Plutonian processes in a way that brings about greater control and organization in the affairs ruled by Pluto, directing that which is truly transformational. Pluto, on the other hand, is going to *Plutonize* Saturn. It's going to try and reform, heal, and transform all things Saturnian, eliminating that which is destructive to Saturn's ultimate goal of perfect form. So, taken together, Saturn-Pluto symbolizes the transformation of structures and the regulation of transformations.

SATURN'S INFLUENCE ON PLUTO

Saturn asks how can Pluto phenomena be better organized and directed toward useful ends? This might mean **regulating processes of regeneration**, such as is occurring right now in debates over legislation to control reproductive **cloning**. Reproductive cloning, as opposed to therapeutic cloning, has to do with the regeneration of cellular structures for purposes of creating a baby. Human cloning is seen by most people as a threat to society; thus, it must be restrained. Therapeutic cloning, however, involves fertilizing a donor egg-cell with a person's DNA for purposes of directing that cell (now an embryo) toward medically useful ends, such as producing pancreatic cells that could cure diabetes. The opposition between Saturn and Pluto is evident in continuing debates over the benefits versus the risks of allowing continued research in this area. "The challenge," says California Senator Diane Feinstein, "is knowing where to strike the balance [opposition] so we don't' end up throwing the baby out with the bathwater."*

It means **finding new and better ways to regulate money management** within corporations. Corporations *incorporate,* meaning they subsume and integrate new businesses into themselves; thus, they are uniquely Plutonian entities. Also, corporations are

---

* Saturn's sign position in Gemini (science) and Pluto's position in Sagittarius (ethics and religion) is evident in the debate over whether cloning violates scientific ethics as well as tenets of the Christian faith. The notion of producing embryos for research has drawn the ire of abortion opponents on religious grounds.

collectively owned by investors through stockholdings, thus they are collective entities as well.* The government—Saturn—has been forced to find new ways to regulate corporations in the wake of the unlawful and destructive practices that have become increasingly apparent after the Enron scandal. By casting a cool and critical eye on Enron's debris and those who made it, government (Saturn) can strengthen our economic system (Pluto). Accordingly, a slew of public policy proposals have recently been advanced that are designed to reform corporate culture for the better.

The Enron scandal is just one of many examples of what can happen when Pluto is unregulated by Saturn. Insufficient integration between these two planets is apt to show up as situations wherein Plutonic processes are careening out of control, e.g., rampant greed in corporations. Much poisonous corporate behavior is facilitated by inappropriate laws or condoned by the absence of laws, i.e., *deregulation*. The complete lack of appropriate enforcement and nonexistent federal regulation, which was essentially purchased via campaign contributions to lawmakers, allowed Enron to manipulate an energy crisis in California. It has come to light that energy traders for Enron used ruthless schemes with nicknames like "Death Star" to manipulate California's electricity market and boost profits.** Internal company documents constitute proof that California's power debacle was caused by Enron looking to make money rather than by actual energy shortages. Accordingly, there is now a federal criminal investigation focusing on fraud, racketeering, and conspiracy.

Additional controls include **new rules for the accounting**

---

* Pluto is a collective, or transpersonal planet in that it has to do with forces beyond the personal. Hence, it is associated with things like the economy-at-large, mob rule, revolts, populist uprisings, and any other phenomena produced by the masses.

** The moniker "Death Star" is particularly damning in that it's a metaphor drawn from the ultra-evil space station in "Star Wars IV" that was used to dominate and, if necessary, destroy planets that refused to pay ransom to the evil Empire.

industry. Anderson's role in the Enron debacle has shined a new light on fraudulent accounting practices. As consultants, Anderson was providing financial advice to Enron while also auditing Enron's books, which is a clear conflict of interest. Accordingly, the SEC has proposed a "no-nonsense" watchdog panel with the power to investigate, discipline, and publicize abuses in the accounting industry, which has been self-regulated until now. This has led to a complete overhaul of accounting rules. The SEC is also investigating conflicts of interest among stock analysts that work for major banks, like Merrill Lynch. These are financial researchers and analysts who end up recommending the purchase of stocks that actually line their own pockets; thus, they can't be objective or impartial in the advice they give investors. As a result, the SEC has approved **new ethics rules for stock analysts** that are designed to prevent such conflicts of interest from arising.

Pluto's sign position, Sagittarius, which rules ethics and justice, has clearly been a factor. So much corruption and scandal has been uncovered within Wall Street that it's created **a boon for corporate lawyers**. In the current post-Enron climate, there is a profound lack of trust among investors due to inaccurate corporate reporting of holdings and performance. Disillusioned investors who have been scammed by unscrupulous practices within the banking and finance industry are suing in unprecedented numbers. Heightened sensitivity and awareness of corruption is causing legal reform, spearheaded by Washington and various regulatory agencies that oversee ethical and responsible practices to protect the public.

The crisis and corruption at Enron helped to push the **campaign finance reform** bill "over the top." Enron provided such a clear example of how big money can influence government (Enron lobbied for deregulation of the power industry, and Washington complied) that the government has been forced to *finally* institute controls on "soft money" contributions that have corrupted governmental process. The Campaign Finance Reform bill represents the largest overhaul of campaign spending rules since the Watergate scandals a generation ago.

Yet another area that involves governmental controls on money flows involve the treasury department, which has **frozen the funds** of numerous entities suspected of financing terrorist organizations. This is a perfect example of Saturn-Pluto. Saturn, of course, involves contraction, or "freezing," and Pluto rules financial transactions, thus the freezing of funds.

It almost goes without saying that there has been significant pressure on Alan Greenspan and the Federal Reserve to regulate money flows by lowering interest rates in order to combat the current **economic recession**. The recession is itself an example of Saturn (slowdown, downsizing, contraction) and Pluto (investments, risk taking).

BRING EVIL UNDER CONTROL

In myriad ways, there's been a focus on trying to bring evil (Pluto) under control (Saturn). These include building an international coalition in the war on terrorism; stockpiling vaccines to increase our readiness to deal with biological attack; strengthening the Intelligence Community so that our country can be better secured against criminal elements and foreign invaders; restraining the rampant greed of corporations like Enron and making them more accountable; mandating new policies for reporting incidents of child sexual abuse in the church; preventing rogue scientists from creating human clones; keeping child porn off the internet; amending the constitution to protect the rights of crime victims; establishing a new federal reimbursement code for Medicare that will allow doctors to identify themselves as specialists in pain management; and trying former Yugoslav President Slobodan

Milosevic on charges of genocide and crimes against humanity.*
All of these examples illustrate ways that Saturn has attempted to
regulate actual or potential Plutonic excesses during this period of
Pluto opposing Saturn.

THE DARK FATHER

If Saturn is father, and Pluto darkness, then Saturn-Pluto *can* be
the dark father—or, as George Lucas would have, *Darth Vader.* Of
late we've had more than our usual share of this sorry lot. Examples: Osama Bin Laden who laughed in recounting how his young
Arab men in America did not know they were on a suicide mission
until just before they boarded the plane, Enron CEO Kenneth Lay
who encouraged his employees to buy more Enron stock while he
was selling off shares as fast as he could in anticipation of Enron's
imminent collapse, Father John Geoghan of Boston who molested
some 130 boys under his care, and Iraq President Sadaam Hussein who offers thousands of dollars to Palestinian families whose
children become suicide bombers (thus financing the death of Palestinian youths).

These are just some of the examples of dark fathers that we've
been reading about this past year. The good news, if there is any
in this sorry litany of human ruin, is that all save Hussein (and his
time may be near) are paying a dear price for their crimes.

RULES FOR DYING

Finding ways to manage death & dying is yet another Saturn-
Pluto theme. In January, the Supreme Court agreed to decide a
challenge to the constitutionality of the death penalty laws in nine
states where judges, rather than juries, determine whether to sen-
tence a killer to death. More than 700 death sentences could be

---

* This would make Milosevic the first head of state to be taken to count on allegations of genocide, the most grievous of all war crimes.

in question. Conversely, in April a federal judge upheld Oregon's law *allowing* physician-assisted suicide, or Euthanasia, ruling that the Justice Department, headed by John Ashcroft, does not have the authority to overturn it. Significantly, at the same time the federal judge upheld Oregon's law, the Netherlands became the first country in Europe to decriminalize euthanasia, thereby giving patients the right to die. A month later, Belgium passed a similar statute. It's interesting to note that where forced death (execution) seems to be decreasing, the option to exercise control over one's own death (the right to die) is increasing.

PLUTO'S INFLUENCE ON SATURN

Many of the same phenomena that symbolize Saturn's attempts to regulate Pluto can also be interpreted as Pluto's attempt to transform Saturn. Again, the Saturn-Pluto opposition symbolizes (1) the transformation of structures and (2) the regulation of transformations. The same events, in other words, have both properties; you can look at them either way. The main difference is that Saturn represents processes of change from the top down, whereas Pluto symbolizes processes of change from the bottom up. In an integrated opposition, they meet in the middle and complement one another.

Pluto's transformational impact upon Saturn will be threefold: (1) to *penetrate* and *expose* wrongdoing, inefficiency, and mismanagement within organizations; (2) to *purge* and *eliminate* that which is destructive to Saturnian systems; and (3) to *reform* and *integrate* disparate elements in order to bring about greater complexity, integrity, and power within a given structure.

With Pluto, transformational change is initiated from deep within, from the underworld, from the oppressed disempowered elements of the system. This includes adults molested as children who sue the Catholic Church, enraged Enron shareholders who lost billions of dollars as the company tumbled into bankruptcy, desperate Palestinians humiliated by Israeli occupation, and Arab youth sickened and twisted by the inability of their governments to fully embrace modernization and provide them with a sense of purpose, meaning, and hope—forcing them to turn, instead, to Islamic fundamentalism. Eventually, these shadow elements rise up and attack the existing Saturnian order. They symbolize the return of the repressed.

ELIMINATING EVIL & STRENGTHENING DEFENSE

On the one hand, you can look at the war on terrorism as a Saturnian attempt to suppress evildoers and avert danger by building an international coalition with stringent laws, rules, and regulations. *Or*, you can look at al Qaeda, the Taliban, and Islamic fundamentalism as ultra-Saturnian organizations—tyrannical, rigid, and oppressive—that have to be eliminated. Counterterrorism is our Plutonian response to purge evildoers from the planetary body in the same way that antibodies attack foreign invaders and flush them from a human body. It is an immune system response to a toxic Saturnian element that has become extreme in its destructiveness to the integrity of the geopolitical system.*

While counterterrorism signifies an effort to reform the

---

* It is remarkable how terrorism is also coming to light within our own country. Last summer, just prior to the first Saturn-Pluto opposition, Timothy McVay was executed in Oklahoma. McVay was responsible for the worst terrorist attack on U.S. soil prior to September 11th. Bobby Frank Cherry was convicted of murder on May 22, 2002; just days before the final Saturn-Pluto pass on the 25th. Cherry is the former Klansman who is accused of planting the bomb in 1963 that killed four black girls inside a church to Birmingham. It was the deadliest attack against the Civil Rights movement at that time. Also on trial this year are four former Symbionese Liberation Army members who murdered a woman in a deadly 1975-bank robbery. Their trial is the latest chapter in the 1974 kidnapping of the newspaper heiress, Patricia Hearst, certainly the most famous terrorist act of that era. This past January, one of the four members, Sarah Jane Olsen, who was captured in 1999, pleaded guilty to trying to bomb two L.A. police cars. Saturn is about accountability; Pluto is about terrorism. So with the opposition, it's time suffer the consequences of one's violent acts. This is the lesson of Saturn. Clearly, these are bad times for terrorists.

world culture, reforms are also taking place within our national government, especially the FBI, CIA, and INS. Mismanagement and administrative lapses have proved not only embarrassing to these organizations, but also lethal to the citizens they are pledged to protect. FBI Director Robert Mueller announced in December that the bureau is being completely reorganized to strengthen the agency's ability to deter terrorist attacks. In particular, the bureau's manpower and resources are being expanded and refocused on intelligence-gathering capabilities. Here again we see evidence of Gemini/Sagittarius (intelligence gathering and hypothesis formation) in the service of empowering national security systems (Saturn-Pluto).

In a May speech before Congress, Mueller captures the essence of Saturn-Pluto. "Terrorists have shown they are willing to go to great lengths to destroy America," Mueller told senators. "We must be willing to go to even greater lengths to stop them. Our worldwide network must be more powerful. Our financial commitment must be stronger. Our techniques, training and technology must be more sophisticated. And our sense of urgency and intensity must be greater."

In December, 2001, the House passed an Intelligence bill to strengthen the CIA by placing new emphasis on human spy networks. The goal is to provide better training and funding to empower CIA agents to infiltrate suspected terrorist organizations throughout the world.

And finally, there have been sweeping reforms within the INS this past month (April, 2002). The entire agency has been transformed into two separate agencies—one to handle immigration services—determining who to let into America—and the other for law enforcement—pursuing and prosecuting aliens who violate the laws of America. INS reforms include creating several new administrative (Saturn) positions for overseeing and coordinating the agency's border patrol efforts, increasing the security of our national borders by upping the number of immigration inspectors, toughening enforcement of immigration laws, keeping better track of foreign students, and providing a new database that will allow the FBI and CIA to coordinate intelligence information with the INS to help in screening visa applicants and foreigners entering the United States.

INTEGRATION EQUALS GLOBALIZATION

An unintended consequence of the war on terror is that it's led to an unprecedented degree of cooperation within the world community. At the broadest level, there has been a reordering of the international system. Various governments are working together to make arrests, share intelligence, shut down safe houses, close bank accounts, track money laundering, halt drug trafficking (which finances terrorism), and pursue international criminals literally to the ends of the earth. In effect, there is a massive flushing out of crime and a purging of evil on a global scale. Of course, it would be naïve to assume any final solution to such problems, but it does seem that the global immune system has become massively strengthened over the past year (2002).

As mentioned, power is a function of a system's integrity, i.e., its degree of integration: the greater the integration, the greater the power. This is what's happening globally; were integrating. I've already mentioned the end of the cold war and the inclusion of Russia as a NATO ally, which is historic to say the least. For all its troubles, Saturn-Pluto has had an integrative, transformational effect on the world. We are increasingly becoming, in the words of Marshall McLuhan, a global village. Again, this is the essence of Saturn-Pluto: a process of integration in which disparate parts unite to form a new, more complex, geo-political whole. This process can be summed in the buzzword for the times: *globalization*.

Another example supporting this trend is the introduction of the European Union (EU) Eurodollar, which premiered in January. Twelve countries, all of which had different currencies before 2002, now have *one*. The distribution of some $600 billion worth of euros together with the collection of a roughly equal amount of the former currencies makes this the largest currency change in history. The new money is said to be a symbol of Europe's increasing economic and political integration. It is also an apt symbol for the Saturn-Pluto opposition; Saturn rules politics, Pluto rules economics, and opposition has brought them together in cooperative harmony.

PURGING THE CHURCH

I've mentioned how legal enforcement of new rules for reporting child sexual abuse are forcing Catholic Church officials to be held accountable for charges of sexual abuse by pedophile priests. This is change from the top down, i.e., Saturn regulating Pluto. From Pluto's perspective, however, the church itself is an organization that must be reformed and purged of its destructive elements. Whereas Saturn demands accountability, Pluto demands elimination. Again, the Plutonic healing impulse comes from within the church itself, i.e., from the church's oppressed and traumatized children who, having grown up, confronted the authorities that violated their trust. It's essentially a populist movement to expose abuses of authority.

Catholics throughout the country are uniting in their opposition to the secrecy and mismanagement that has exacerbated the crisis. Reform movements are springing up across the nation, demanding that the litany of Catholic bishops who have confessed to covering up the problem be removed. To date, only those bishops actually accused of molesting children have been forced to resign. Those caught in the cover-ups, such as Cardinals Roger Mahoney of Los

Angeles and Bernard Law of Boston, have ignored critics calling for their removal. However, like death, Pluto is inexorable in its process of elimination. It would seem that sooner or later those clerics that protected their brother-priests, rather than children, must be flushed from the system like toxic waste.

INTEGRATING THE CHURCH'S SHADOW

Pluto also signifies a process of integration within the church. It's no surprise that the church's shadow is sexuality and, by implication, woman. While criminal convictions of priests who molested children may have a purging effect on the Catholic Church, it has also reawakened the debate surrounding clerical celibacy and disallowance of woman in the priesthood.

In the West, the rule of celibacy was not established churchwide until the 12th century. Later, it was set as the Roman Catholic official discipline at the Council of Trent in 1563. In my opinion, however, enforced celibacy creates a breeding ground for perversion. Individuals are not allowed to mature sexually, with the result that they may seek an immature sexual outlet—children—that reflects their own arrested development. If sexual energy is denied legitimate expression, it tends to seek illegitimate ways to gratify itself. The choice of a forbidden sexual object, e.g., a young boy, reflects a priest's self-imposed prohibition against his own sexual impulses. Accordingly, Catholic dissidents are calling for radical reforms within the Church that would pressure the pope to integrate sexuality into church doctrine by (1) repealing the requirement of celibacy, and (2) allowing woman to become priests.

REGENERATION OF LIVING STRUCTURES

One of the most promising examples of a Pluto-Saturn process of reciprocal influence has to do with cloning technologies. At the heart of this movement is our understanding of the structure of the human genome, the mapping of which has recently been completed. The structure of the DNA molecule is arguably *the* most important structure in life. Over the past year (2002) there's been a breakthrough in our understanding of how to extract DNA from the nucleus of a single cell, inject it into a unfertilized human egg cell, and direct the growth of that cell toward useful medical ends, like generating blood vessels that can replace diseased arteries. This is popularly called "therapeutic cloning." For the first time in human history we are able to create a proto-human life form—a fertilized egg cell—that empowers us to regenerate cells that are lost in many incurable diseases.

Called "regenerative medicine," the use of stem cells is controversial because stem-cells come from human embryos, i.e., fertilized egg cells. Embryonic stem cells are the ancestral cells of every cell in the body. In a developing embryo, they *transform* into cells that make up the organs, bone, skin and other tissues. Researchers are learning *to direct (Saturn) the transformation (Pluto)* of such cells to repair hearts, livers, brains and other organs and to treat ailments like cancer, diabetes, and Alzheimer's disease. This process of directing or controlling a transformational process for purposes of regenerating living tissue and healing disease is about as perfect an expression of Saturn-Pluto as one could hope to find.

REGENERATION OF THE FEDERAL GOVERNMENT

Speaking of regeneration, a somewhat grim example involved the Bush administration's efforts to create what's been called a "shadow" government—an apt term for Saturn-Pluto. After the September 11th attack, the government dispatched about 100 civilian managers to live and work at two fortified secret locations on the East Coast. These people effectively amount to a "second team" government, a rotating group of officials representing key departments and agencies that will step in and assume power, i.e., regenerate government, in the event of a nuclear attack on Washington. Each one has to do what's called "bunker duty," live and work underground 24 hours a day for shifts as long as 90 days. Pluto, of course, rules the underground, and Saturn (government) is literally there!

REGENERATION OF ARAB COUNTRIES

Studies reveal that countries with the most economic freedom also have the highest rates of long- term economic growth. Also, economically free countries exhibit greater tolerance and civility than economically repressed ones, where feelings of hopelessness, impotence, and isolation foment fanaticism and terrorism. According to some experts, the one great cause of the rise of Islamic fundamentalism is the total failure of political institutions in the Arab World. The main problem with Arab countries is their refusal to make the transition to modernity, i.e., to join the global community, open up their societies, allow for political parties and free elections, embrace a free market economy, and implement the rule of law.

A terrible consequence of this failure is a population of frustrated, embittered, discontented young men brainwashed by religious schools that divert their rage from revolt against their own governments to hatred of non-Muslim societies. It's essentially a sour grapes attitude. Islam is being taken over by a small poisonous element—fundamentalists—who advocate cruel and repressive attitudes toward woman, education, the economy, and modern life in general.

Islamic Fundamentalism *is* a reform movement, but it is *reactionary* reform. The conservative, rigid values of Islamic fundamentalism are polarized to the progressive, liberal values of the west. Rather than change with the times, they have regressed and become entrenched in an 11th century medieval value system that promises certainty in times of bewildering confusion. Fundamentalism looks backward rather than forward, is simple rather than complex, exclusive rather than inclusive.

The west has supported the status quo in many of these countries because it's been fearful of unsettling the domestic situation and jeopardizing the continued production of oil, upon which we depend. However, by ignoring human rights violations and the oppressive, deadening despair produced by state run economies, America has inadvertently fed the growth of terrorist groups like al Qaeda.

The antidote to the virus of fundamentalism is to *redirect* a revolutionary process that is already occurring within these countries. This means pressuring Arab regimes to open up their society. The Pluto watchword, again, is *reform*, cultural and political transformation. Experts agree the free word must help closed societies join the international community; i.e., we must *integrate* them. Of course, this will take many, many years, but the Saturn-Pluto opposition is signaling it's time for a "declaration of interdependence"—a vision of global unity which acknowledges that no one nation can experience full prosperity until others have prosperity as well.

Various strategies for bringing reform to inept regimes include linking foreign aid to a country's willingness to end corruption and open up their economies. In a recent address to a summit of 50 nations gathered for a conference on global aid, President Bush called on the world's wealthy nations to budget their foreign aid more tightly to reforms. "The lesson of our time is clear," he said. "When nations close their markets and opportunity is hoarded by a privileged view, no amount – no amount – of development aid is ever enough. We must tie greater aid to political and legal and economic reforms. And by insisting on reform, we do the work of compassion."

Other strategies for promoting reforms include funding moderate Muslim groups and scholars, thus enabling them to broadcast fresh thinking across the Arab world aimed at breaking the power of the fundamentalists. Experts also insist that we push these governments to modernize their education systems and allow for a free press. This strategy seems particularly appropriate given that Saturn-Pluto is in the learning/teaching signs, Gemini and Sagittarius.

SUMMARY

Saturn-Pluto is not just about suicide bombers, pedophile priests, and corrupt CEO's, it's also an occasion for world transformation. While there is always a certain degree of corruption, inefficiency, greed, fear, evil, and paranoia in the world, it is when Saturn-Pluto comes into opposition that these problems are thrust fully into the limelight. Symptoms become flagrant and obvious, and cry out for a solution. It's amazing when you think about it: 911. That's the number we call when there's an emergency. A condition of urgent need suddenly emerges into awareness that requires action. Saturn-Pluto is signaling its time to clean out the stables.

The Saturn-Pluto opposition has signified an evolutionary period of development. On the one hand, it's been a time for managing crises, bringing evil under control, confronting abuses of power, and bolstering defenses against destructive entities. It's also been a time for regenerating life through new technologies like stem-cell research, and for completing long overdue reforms within business and government. These include a reformulation of foreign policy to heal the underlying causes of terrorism, a purging of individuals and groups that are harmful to the public interest, elimination of corporate policies that foster greed and corruption, and the integration of disparate elements to create organizations, and ultimately a world-order, which is more humane, unified, and conducive to the public good. In short, the Saturn-Pluto opposition has been a time for the transformation of structures and the regulation of transformations.

Surely, this is not all bad. It seems to me that there is a profound intelligence operating in these events, a divine intent, or cosmic plan. The poet Christopher Fry writes, "Thank God, our time is now. When wrong comes up to meet us everywhere, never to leave us till we take the longest stride of soul men ever took." The wonderful thing about astrology is that it shines a light on the nature of this "stride" and helps us to see its underlying purpose and direction. It enables us to see that our suffering does indeed have meaning, that Saturn-Pluto is it is own prescription for the world's ills, and that we can assist the healing process by trusting and aligning ourselves with it.

ENDNOTES

Chapter 1

1 Jung, C.G. (1953). *Two essays on Analytical Psychology.* Collected Works, Vol. 7, Bollingen Series XX., p. 92. New York: Pantheon.
2 Ibid, p. 78
3 Jung, C.G. (1933). *Modern man in search of a soul.*, p. 35.
4 Abrams, J. (1991). *Meeting the shadow,* p. 304
5 Ibid, p. xxv
6 Guggenbuhl-Craig, A. (1971). *Power in the helping professions,* (p. 94)
7 Harvey, J. & Katz, C. (1984). *If I'm so successful, why do I feel like a fake?*
8 Guggenbuhl-Craig, A. (1971), p. 110

Chapter 2

1 In *San Francisco Chronicle, Datebook,* January 26, 1997, p. 30.
2 In US Online News, February 7, 1999.
3 *Vanity Fair,* September 1998, p. 309.
4 *Vanity Fair,* September 1998, p. 328.
5 *Vanity Fair,* September 1998, p. 329.
6 *Biography,* May 1997, p. 70.
7 *Vanity Fair,* September 1998, p. 328.
8 *Vanity Fair,* September 1998, p. 309.
9 *Biography,* May 1997, p. 71.
10 *Biography,* May 1997, p. 71.
11 *Vanity Fair,* September 1998, p. 328.
12 Quoted in *Dr. Laura: The Unauthorized Biography*, by Vickie Bane,1999, p. 79.
13 *Newsweek,* March 20, 2000, p. 52.
14 "Canada Rebukes Dr. Laura for Anti-Gay Statements," By Colin Nickerson, *San Francisco Chronicle,* May 12, 2000, p. C2.
15 In a June 9th and December 21st , 1999 radio show.
16 *Vanity Fair,* September 1998, p. 308-9.
17 *US Online News,* Feb 27, 1999.
18 "Dr. Laura, Talk Radio Celebrity," *Newsweek,* March 20, 2000, p. 52
19 "It's time to bear arms," *Jewish World Review,* Sept. 22, 1999 /12 Tishrei, 5760
20 "It's time to bear arms," *Jewish World Review,* Sept. 22, 1999 /12 Tishrei, 5760
21 Times of London, "'Protest at anti-gay TV host," March 22, 2000
22 *San Francisco Sunday Examiner & Chronicle, Datebook,* January 26, 1997, p. 30.
23 *San Francisco Sunday Examiner & Chronicle, Datebook,* January 26, 1997, p. 30.
24 *Vanity Fair,* September 1998, p. 328.
25 "Dr. Laura's Dirty Dozen," on the www.clublove.com Website operated by Internet Entertainment Group ((IEG), Oct. 22, 1998.
26 Vanity Fair, September 1998, p. 329.
27 "Why Celebrate Homosexuality?" Jewish World Review July 27, 1999 /14 Av, 5759
28 "Why Celebrate Homosexuality?" Jewish World Review July 27, 1999 /14 Av, 5759
29 "'Animal Farm' lessons relevant as ever," Jewish World Review Nov. 16, 1999 /7 Kislev, 5760

50 "It's time to bear arms," *Jewish World Review,* Sept. 22, 1999 /12 Tishrei, 5760
51 "Cybersex survey a travesty of science," *Jewish World Review,* May 3, 1999 / 17 Iyar 5759
52 Guggenbuhl-Craig, A. (1971). *Power in the helping professions.* Dallas, TX: Spring Publications.
53 In *Vanity Fair,* September 1998, p. 329
54 Ibid.

Chapter 3

1   Handy, Bruce, "The Force Is Back," *Time,* February 10, 1997, p. 74.
2   Williams, Joanne. "Sun Interviews George Lucas," *Pacific Sun,* February 8, 1980, p. 7.
3   Pye, Michael and Myles, Lynda (1979), *The Movie Brats,* New York: Holt, Rinehart, and Winston, p. 9.
4   Chutkow, Paul, "The Lucas Chronicles," Image Magazine in the *San Francisco Chronicle,* March 21, 1993, p. 15.
5   Yarish, Alice, "George Lucas—hell-raiser to millionaire," *Independent Journal* (Marin County, CA), March 2, 1980, p. 14.
6   Chutkow, Paul, "The Lucas Chronicles," Image Magazine in the *San Francisco Chronicle,* March 21, 1993, p. 15.
7   Weinraub, Bernard, "Luke Skywalker Goes Home," Playboy Magazine, July, 1997, p. 174.
8   Ibid, p. 12.
9   Handy, Bruce, "The Force Is Back," *Time,* February 10, 1997, p. 72.
10 Weinraub, Bernard, "Luke Skywalker Goes Home," Playboy Magazine, July, 1997, p. 120.
11 Williams, Joanne. "Sun Interviews George Lucas," *Pacific Sun,* February 8, 1980, p. 7.
12 Weinraub, Bernard, "Luke Skywalker Goes Home," Playboy Magazine, July, 1997, p. 176.
13 Brooks, Terry (1999), *Star Wars, Episode I, The Phantom Menace,* New York: Ballantine, p. 188.
14 Brooks, Terry (1999), *Star Wars, Episode I, The Phantom Menace,* New York: Ballantine, p. 191.
15 Brooks, Terry (1999), *Star Wars, Episode I, The Phantom Menace,* New York: Ballantine, p. 322.
16 Salvatore, R.A. (2002), *Star Wars, Episode II, Attack of The Clones,* New York: Ballantine, p. 271-272.
17 Salvatore, R.A. (2002), *Star Wars, Episode II, Attack of The Clones,* New York: Ballantine, p. 274-278.
18 Salvatore, R.A. (2002), *Star Wars, Episode II, Attack of The Clones,* New York: Ballantine, p. 283.
19 Chutkow, Paul, "The Lucas Chronicles," Image Magazine in the *San Francisco Chronicle,* March 21, 1993, p. 15.
20 Handy, Bruce, "The Force Is Back," *Time,* February 10, 1997, p. 73.
21 Chutkow, Paul, "The Lucas Chronicles," Image Magazine in the *San Francisco Chronicle,* March 21, 1993, p. 16.
22 Ibid, p. 10.

CHAPTER 4

1.   Cotta Vaz, Mark, (2005), *Living dangerously: The adventures of Merian C. Cooper,* New York: Random House
2.   Cotta Vaz, Mark. *Living dangerously,* p. 5).
3.   Ibid. p. 236.
4.   Cooper, M., and Wallace, E. (1932). *King Kong.* Nevada City, CA. Underwood Books, p. 105.
5.   Cotta Vaz, Mark, quoting Cooper in *Living dangerously,* p. 186.
6.   *King Kong,* p. 28.
7.   Jung, C. "A Review of The Complex Theory," in *The Structure and Dynamics of the Psyche,* C.W., 8.
8.   Jung, C. "The Psychological Foundations of the Belief in Spirits," in *The Structure and Dynamics of the Psyche,* C.W., 8. p. 311.
9.   Ibid. p. 92.
10. Campbell, J. (1959). *The masks of god.* New York: Viking Press, Inc., p. 170.
11. Bird, C., and Brownlow, K. (2005). *I'm King Kong: The exploits of Marian C. Cooper.* Documentary film.
12. Jung, Ibid. p. 311.

REFERENCES

Abrams, J. (1991). Epilogue. In C. Zweig and J. Abrams (Eds.), *Meeting the shadow.* Los Angeles, Jeremy Tarcher.

Guggenbuhl-Craig, A. (1971). *Power in the helping professions.* Dallas, TX: Spring Publications.

Guggenbuhl-Craig, A. (1991). Quacks, charlatans, and false prophets. In C. Zweig and J. Abrams (Eds.), *Meeting the shadow.* Los Angeles, Jeremy Tarcher.

Harvey, J. & Katz, C. (1984). *If I'm so successful, why do I feel like a fake? The imposter phenomenon.* New York: Saint Martins Press.

Jung, C.G. (1933). *Modern man in search of a soul.* New York: Harcourt & Brace.

Jung, C.G. (1953). *Two essays on Analytical Psychology.* Collected Works, Vol. 7, Bollingen Series XX., pp. 78, 190-193. New York: Pantheon.

Zweig, C., & Abrams, J. (1991). *Meeting the shadow.* Los Angeles: Jeremy Tarcher.